A.J.A. SYMONS

A.J.A. SYMONS

A BIBLIOMANE, HIS BOOKS,
AND HIS CLUBS

SIMON C. W. HEWETT

NEW YORK
THE GROLIER CLUB
2018

CATALOGUE OF

AN EXHIBITION HELD AT THE GROLIER CLUB

NOVEMBER 7, 2018 – JANUARY 5, 2019

CONTENTS

ACKNOWLEDGMENTS

I was introduced to A.J.A. Symons by my friend Michael Steele in 1973 when he gave me a copy of *A.J.A. Symons: His Life and Speculations* by Julian Symons, and I wish to acknowledge Michael as the grandfather of this exhibition. I would also like to thank Fern Cohen, Chair of the Committee on Members' Exhibitions, and Chris Loker, Chair of the Publications Committee, for guiding me through the necessary process for mounting such an exhibition at the Grolier Club, and Caroline Schimmel and Mark Samuels Lasner for their interest in this exhibition.

Janice Fisher and Jerry Kelly, respectively, edited and designed this catalogue, making very significant improvements. I am most grateful to them.

Jennifer B. Lee of the Rare Book & Manuscript Library of Columbia University, Curtis Small of Special Collections at the University of Delaware Library, Ed and Ben Maggs of Maggs Bros. Ltd., and Jim Cummins and Henry Wessells of James Cummins Bookseller were also most helpful as I researched Symons.

Finally, I would like to thank my wife, Marjorie, and my son, Christopher, for putting up with my fascination with this remarkable person, A.J.A. Symons.

Ever gratefully

A.J.A. Symons

I

A.J.A. SYMONS
A SUMMARY BIOGRAPHY

Bibliophile, bibliographer, bookdealer, calligrapher, serial club founder, gourmet, author, biographer, and expert on Baron Corvo, Oscar Wilde, and Victorian musical boxes, A.J.A. Symons – now best remembered as the author of *The Quest for Corvo*, published in 1934 – achieved an extraordinary amount in his 41 years. Desmond Flower, the publisher and author who collaborated with Symons on a number of projects, considered Symons "the most remarkable man in the world of letters in [Great Britain] of the period between the wars."[1]

Symons, who once said of himself that "no-one so poor has lived so well,"[2] was born in South London in August 1900, thereby becoming a very late entrant to the Victorian era that he so loved. His father, a Russian Jewish immigrant who took the name Morris Symons, was a dealer in secondhand furniture who became prosperous following his acquisition of London's Moorgate Auction Rooms early in World War One, only to lose his fortune by 1921. Fortunately, during the war, Morris Symons had bought Mount Lebanon, a 20-room house at 9 Cedars Road, Clapham, London, which was to remain the family's base and, frequently, Symons's own base for the rest of his life. Symons's mother, Minnie Bull, was English, with French and Spanish antecedents.

The Symons family included four sons, of whom Alphonse James Albert, or A.J., as Symons preferred to be called, was the eldest, and a daughter. His youngest brother, Julian, became a leading writer of crime fiction, as well as Symons's biographer. Morris Symons, the second son, was also an author, writing a book on table tennis in 1935 and then three detective novels in the sixties.

Symons was educated locally, left school at the age of 14, and was then apprenticed to a furrier. Symons described those three years as a period of drudgery but also of self-education, and during this time he determined to mix "with people who, by the chance of fortune and education, were on the plane to which I had, by my own efforts, raised myself."[3] In 1918, Symons joined the Artists Rifles, a London Regiment in the British army, as a private. He was not a success in the army, did not see active service, and was demobbed in 1919.

Symons then went to work for his father in the Moorgate Auction Rooms until their sale in 1921. He developed some experience in the sale of books and also taught himself calligraphy by copying pages from the *Dictionary of National Biography*.[4] He also met Captain Harold Fisher, who became an intimate and a lifelong friend, and who encouraged Symons's interest in the exploration of Africa as well as assisting Symons on his planned bibliography of late Victorian writers. Symons's 1928 book *Emin* was dedicated to Fisher.

Through his work at the Moorgate Auction Rooms, Symons also met Max Judge, the son of a leading architect, with whom, upon Morris Symons's sale of the Auction Rooms, and Symons's consequent loss of employment, he first entered a short and unprofitable partnership dealing in books and furniture. Subsequently, however, Symons assisted Judge with the lucrative termination of Judge's office lease, before joining Judge in another unsuccessful partnership, this time as bettors on horse races. Symons and Judge then founded The First Edition Club, which was registered on June 30, 1922. The Club operated out of a room at 17 Pall Mall East. Judge was described in the prospectus as the Club's Principal, and Symons was employed as its Director and Secretary, at a salary of £4 a week.

The initial prospectus stated that the Club had been formed with the "primary object of providing a book service that shall also be a first edition service" and that it would seek to be in a position "to supply members with first editions of all books they order, when ordinary book channels would fail them." A later prospectus, dating from after the Club's move to Bedford Square in 1928 described below, states that "The First Edition Club was founded in 1922 by Mr. A.J.A. Symons to provide a meeting-place for those who love fine books of all kinds." Max Judge, who had co-founded and financed the Club, was, however, included at the top of the list of the Club's benefactors for housing the

Club during its first year. In a later printing of that prospectus in 1929, Judge is recognized for having "assisted in the founding of the Club" and for serving as "Chairman of Committee" for some months, but the reference to housing the Club has been dropped, and Judge has been moved down to near the bottom of the list of benefactors.

Percy Muir, a leading London antiquarian bookseller, believed, however, that the Club "aimed, in fact, at short-circuiting the antiquarian bookseller by buying and selling to its members, while pretending to be a disinterested organization at the service of collectors."[5] This view is supported by certain of the original Objects of the Club, including intent to obtain scarce and out-of-print books, to represent members at book auctions, and to facilitate the exchange of duplicate copies of first editions or other "collector's books." Muir also noted that Symons had a reputation in the book trade of not paying for his purchases.[6] Desmond Flower referenced the controversy surrounding Symons's bookselling activities in his autobiography *Fellows in Foolscap*, stating that one bookseller had only agreed to send a book on approval provided that Flower assure him that he was not in business with Symons.[7]

James Laver recounts in *Museum Piece* that Vyvyan Holland (a bibliophile and the younger and surviving son of Oscar Wilde) told him that "when Symons started The First Edition Club he knew almost nothing of first editions . . . But he learned, and he learned quickly."[8] Symons himself stated in "The Book-Collector's Apology," an article in the first number of *The Book-Collector's Quarterly*, that he became a book collector at the age of 14 "by the simple act of buying two different Lives of Shelley. I read them both and, noting contradictions, desired a third. It was then that the shadow of the 'first edition' fell across my path."[9] Symons states that as he grew older, his acquisitions became numerous, and in about 1919 he prepared a manuscript catalogue of his collection listing 163 titles and commissioned a bookplate for his collection at Mount Lebanon.

In December 1922, the Club held its First Loan Exhibition, which included some remarkable books lent by a number of its members. Lacking space to exhibit in its clubroom on Pall Mall East, the Club held the exhibition in the house of Mrs. Cohen, one of its members. An elaborate catalogue prepared by Symons accompanied the exhibition, and this was to be both the first of the Club's 24 publications and the first of Symons's own publications.

The Club had too small a membership to cover its costs, and in May 1923, following cumulative losses of £200, Judge made over his interest in The First Edition Club to Symons, who thus became its sole owner. At that time, the Club had only 60[10] members, and although based on Pall Mall East, conducted its limited operations from a single room. However, among the friends that Symons had made through the Club were the Foyle brothers, owners of Foyles Bookshop, who in July 1923 became 50 percent owners and financial backers of the Club, permitting the continuation of Symons's salary.

The Club itself now relocated to 69 Great Russell Street, and then to 6 Little Russell Street in Bloomsbury. The opening of the new premises was celebrated with a dinner chaired by C. H. St. John Hornby, founder of the Ashendene Press, with toasts by Sir Israel Gollancz and Gordon Selfridge.[11] In 1924, Symons married Victoria ("Gladys") Weeks, a buyer for a fashion house whom he had met while he was in the army. They spent their honeymoon on a somewhat farcical voyage on a small yacht that Symons co-owned with the Foyle brothers, and then set up house at 4 Upper Gloucester Place, London.

A new edition of the Club's Objects and Rules was published from 69 Great Russell Street following the change in ownership, and Symons was now described as the Club's Proprietor and Financial Guarantor; there was, however, no mention of the Foyles. It is notable that none of the Club's six original independent Committee members listed in the initial Objects and Rules issued in 1922 continued to be listed in the 1923 prospectus. Finally, the Club's annual subscription was doubled to one guinea, although the entrance fee was eliminated.

The Club attracted new members, but never as many as Symons hoped for. Nonetheless, by mid-1924, the membership had grown to 200,[12] and it further grew to 367[13] by 1930. Among its distinguished members were leading book collectors, including J. R. Abbey, Lord Esher, Crosby Gaige, Holbrook Jackson, ex-King Manoel of Portugal, and Dr. George Williamson; printers, including C. R. Ashbee (Essex House Press), C. H. St. John Hornby, Francis Meynell (Pelican and Nonesuch presses), Stanley Morison (Monotype Corporation), and Oliver Simon (Curwen Press); authors, including E. F. Benson, Tancred Borenius, Vyvyan Holland, Shane Leslie, and Lytton Strachey; and artists, including Percy Smith and J. Buckland Wright. Perhaps more surprisingly, the membership included four leading retail magnates: Ambrose Heal, Ivor Stewart-Liberty, Robert Sainsbury, and Gordon Selfridge. It was Symons's policy not to permit bookdealers to join, but exceptions were made for Ernest Maggs, C. S. Millard, and A. S. W. Rosenbach. A number of members, particularly Vyvyan Holland, Ivor Stewart-Liberty, and George Williamson, became close friends of Symons and were to play important roles in his life.

Symons actively sought to publicize the Club, and in 1924 contributed an article describing the Club's goals and activities to *The Spectator* as part of a series of articles "intended to interest book collectors and having special reference to the work of the First Edition Club."[14] Similarly, Volume 31 of *Penrose's Annual* (1929) contains a survey of the objects and achievements to that date of the Club by Symons, and is perhaps the most explicit of his writings in stating the Club's emulation of the Grolier Club of New York.[15] Membership of the Club was enhanced by Annual Reunion Dinners. Speakers at the 1929 dinner, for example, included Desmond MacCarthy, Francis Meynell, Michael Sadleir, and Sir Osbert Sitwell, as well as Symons himself.

The Club, however, continued to lose money and in 1927, the Foyle brothers withdrew from the partnership and the Club was incorporated as a limited company owned outright by Symons, with the Foyles receiving payment for their partnership interest in debentures. Symons wanted the Club to offer the comforts of London's older clubs, and sought to acquire a Regency house at 100 Great Russell Street, issuing a lavish pamphlet in an effort to acquire the support and financial backing of its members. At a purchase price of £24,000, and with alterations expected to cost a further £16,000, this was clearly a step too far for so small a club, and instead the lease of a lower-priced but attractive building with Adam features was acquired at 17 Bedford Square. Once refitted, 17 Bedford Square included an Exhibition Room, a tea-room, a garden, a members' dining room, and a flat for Symons as Director of the Club on the second floor. The Club's annual subscription was now increased to five guineas for Town residents and to three guineas for Country members.

The new clubhouse was opened on May 15, 1928, by ex-King Manoel of Portugal. The opening was accompanied by an exhibition of *Selected Examples of Modern English Private Presses,* and was celebrated with another dinner, this time with Dr. George Williamson in the chair and Sir Frederic Kenyon, principal librarian at the British Museum, proposing the toast.[16] Numerous other exhibitions followed, but unfortunately, the Club's social facilities were used by few members other than Symons and his wife. Shane Leslie noted that he hardly met anyone else there – "only A.J. striding about with incessant conversation and holding brilliant exhibitions."[17]

In 1931, *The Book-Collector's Quarterly,* financed by Cassell and co-edited by Symons and Desmond Flower of Cassell, and provided without charge to members of the Club, commenced publication. *The Book-Collector's Quarterly* was published in both a limited and an unlimited format for its first eight numbers. The limited edition copies were printed on handmade paper and included extra illustrations. The first four limited volumes were bound in buckram and the second four in cloth; the first five limited edition volumes were limited to 100 copies, and the last three were limited to 75 copies. From 1933 onward, in order to reduce costs for Cassell, the limited edition copies were discontinued.

By March 1931, Symons was claiming that the Club was recognized by "book collectors all over the world as the European equivalent of the Grolier Club of New York,"[18] but he was also appealing to members for donations to liquidate its debt, and for members to buy from the Club's stock of publications. The acquisition of 17 Bedford Square had been financed by a £5,000 mortgage and through the issuance of £15,000 of debentures, and the Club showed a loss of £2,000 in its first year in its new premises. Although the loss was reduced to £1,500 the following year, it was clear that the Club required additional financing. Symons's solution was to obtain a bank loan of up to £3,500 secured by the pledge of securities owned by Dr. Williamson, the Club's Chairman; Dr. Williamson was to be protected from loss by the guarantees of participating members, including a £500 guarantee from Symons himself.[19]

Nonetheless, in 1931, the Club was wound up, and with the sale of the lease at a loss due to the then-prevailing economic conditions, a significant shortfall ensued. Debenture-holders received only a five percent payout, and the loan guarantees were called. In March 1932, the Club announced its planned return to 6 Little Russell Street, issuing a third prospectus, this time adding that the Club was "The Book-Collector's Club." Symons himself ultimately resolved his guarantee through the sale of books to Dr. Williamson. The assets of the Club were purchased out of bankruptcy by Symons for £500, and the Club resumed operations, albeit on a reduced scale and with an increasingly less active exhibition schedule and publishing program. The activities of the Club wound down in the late thirties as Symons primarily focused on the Wine and Food Society, with *The Book-Collector's Quarterly*, the first 16 numbers of which had been financed by Cassell, ceasing publication with Number 17 in 1935, although a Number 18 had been announced as in preparation, and the last Club publication (*Letters from Aubrey Beardsley to Leonard Smithers*) in 1937. Symons did, however, continue to mount *The Fifty Books of the Year* exhibitions through 1939, and the Club only terminated on Symons's death in 1941.

Despite the Club's financial problems, it made a significant contribution to book-collecting. It published 17 numbers of *The Book-Collector's Quarterly*, which included contributions by Edmund Blunden, Eric Gill, Holbrook Jackson, and D. H. Lawrence, among others; the Club put on over 40 exhibitions of both domestic and foreign books and bookbindings; the Club offered 24 publications to its members, many designed to showcase the capabilities of the designated printers; the Club was a patron of the binder Thomas Harrison, then running the Henry Wood Bindery, and in particular, the Club was an early patron of the Curwen Press; and in 1929 the Club launched its *Fifty*

Books of the Year series, based on the successful US model launched in 1923 by the American Institute of Graphic Arts, which are considered to have helped raise the standards of book production in Britain. Symons contributed an article, "On Selecting the Fifty Books of the Year," to Number VIII of *The Book-Collector's Quarterly* in 1932.

The early publications of the Club tended to be catalogues of exhibitions held by the Club, including catalogues of the First Loan, W. B. Yeats, and Lord Byron exhibitions prepared by Symons himself. Typographical titles included *The Pen and Type-Design* by Graily Hewitt, *The Book of Signs* by Rudolf Koch, *John Bell, 1745–1831* by Stanley Morison, and *Lettering: A Plea* by Percy Smith. A particularly useful title was *A Select Bibliography of the Principal Modern Presses Public and Private in Great Britain and Ireland* by G. S. Tomkinson. In addition, there were titles by Aubrey Beardsley, Ambrose Bierce, Lord Byron, Baron Corvo, Gérard de Nerval, and Jonathan Swift, among others.

A goal of Symons was to highlight the work of the most eminent printers, including Francis Meynell, Stanley Morison, Bernard Newdigate, and Oliver Simon, and the publications were attractively printed by a number of presses, including Curwen Press (12 titles), Cambridge University Press, Chiswick Press, and Oxford University Press (two titles each). Exhibition catalogues were predominantly printed at the Pelican Press.

Almost as interesting as the titles the Club published are those that, while announced, were not. These include an account of Swift's library by Harold Williams, an account of the rarest ancient Irish books by Shane Leslie, two peepshows by modern artists, a biography of Talleyrand by Herbert Trench, *A Bibliography of George Moore* by Symons himself (announced for 1933, and again, more expansively, in 1936), *A Bibliography of the Works of Somerville and Ross* by Elizabeth Hudson (ultimately published in 1942 by the Sporting Gallery and Bookshop in New York, although printed at the Chiswick Press favored by Symons), *Modern Love* by George Meredith, *Tales of Mystery and Imagination* by Edgar Allen Poe, *Selected Essays* by Ambrose Bierce, *Rolfe At Holywell* by Symons (Julian Symons wrote and published this in *The Saturday Book 5* in 1945), and the *Rubaiyat of Omar Khayyam*.

As a result of his involvement in the Club, Symons became known as a bibliophile and as an expert on late Victorian authors. In 1925, he commenced work on *A Bibliography of the Works of the Writers and Book-Illustrators of the Eighteen-Nineties with Short Biographies*. Publication by the Club was announced for 1926, and a prospectus was issued; the book was to be printed under the supervision of Oliver Simon and was to have had an introduction by Holbrook Jackson, with whom Symons had formed a long-lasting friendship. In 1931, the Club announced[20] that the *Bibliography* would be issued in three volumes instead of the originally announced single volume, and at a pre-publication price of six guineas. Unfortunately, although a number of sections were set up in type, and dummy bindings prepared, the book was never completed. In 1928, however, Symons's *An Anthology of "Nineties" Verse* was published by Elkin Mathews & Marrot with a distinctive "nineties" wrapper and binding.

Symons had formed an extensive collection of works and manuscripts by authors of that period, particularly George Moor, Frederick Rolfe (Baron Corvo), and Oscar Wilde, and had developed a friendship with Lord Alfred Douglas, the close friend of Oscar Wilde, printing *Nine Poems* by Douglas in an edition of 50 copies in 1925, and receiving over 300 letters from Douglas over 16 years. Those letters are now in the William Andrews Clark Memorial Library at the University of California, Los Angeles, together with many other letters from Symons. It is a sign of the closeness of Symons's relationship with Douglas that Symons resigned from his London club after being reprimanded by that club's committee for bringing Douglas, who had been in prison, into the club.[21]

Reflecting his knowledge of Wilde, acquired in part through his friendships with Douglas and Vyvyan Holland, in 1927 Symons acted as a defense witness for C. S. Millard, the bookseller and, under the name Stuart Mason, author of *A Bibliography of Oscar Wilde*, in a case involving the purported authorship by Wilde of a play, *For Love of the King*, which Symons believed not to be by Wilde.

In 1928, Symons was contracted by Methuen to write a biography of Wilde, and received a substantial advance. Although several chapters were written, this work too was never to be completed, in part because of objections by Douglas.[22] Symons was, however, able to use projected royalties as partial security for a bank loan. Methuen also explored a new collected edition of Wilde with Symons as editor, and some pieces were set up in proof. A chapter from the proposed biography of Wilde entitled "The Diner-Out" was published in *Fords and Bridges* in 1936 and again by *Horizon* in October 1941. Another chapter, "Wilde at Oxford," appeared in *Horizon* in April 1941. Cyril Connolly, editor of *Horizon*, wrote a postcard to Symons, stating, "Augustus John is enthusiastic about your article. He knew Oscar and says it is exactly like him."[23] Shane Leslie, who had first written of Corvo in the *London Mercury*, thought that Symons "would have written the best Life of Oscar Wilde had he lived."[24]

Symons also collected copies of Wilde's letters with a view to publishing a collected edition, but this project was also not completed. Not until 1962 did Rupert Hart-Davis edit and publish *The Letters of Oscar Wilde*.

In 1926, Dr. Williamson proposed Symons for membership in the Sette of Odd Volumes, a bibliophilic London dining club that had been founded by Bernard Quaritch in 1878. The Sette was limited to 21 members (the number of volumes in the variorum edition of Shakespeare printed in 1821), and up to 21 Supplemental members, and included some of Britain's leading literary and legal personalities. Symons was elected at the 417th meeting on October 26, 1926. Vyvyan Holland had been elected earlier the same year.

The Sette held monthly dinners from October to July, frequently at the Savoy Hotel, or as the Sette put it, "United once a month to form a perfect Sette."[25] Elaborate invitations and menu cards were prepared, frequently designed around the topic of the paper to be delivered at that dinner. There were 21 rules for the Sette, most procedural in nature but including Rule 18: "No Odd Volume shall talk *unasked* on any subject he understands."[26] Jokes were played on members, and Symons himself distributed a mock charge sheet charging Ralph Straus with such offenses as "being found by night in the Savoy Hotel in unlawful possession of writing implements."

In his Inaugural Address on becoming Oddshippe (President) in 1938, Symons described the impact on him of joining the Sette in almost Masonic terms: "To become a member of the Sette of Odd Volumes means to make forty-one new friends; . . . At once I found myself the recipient of numberless acts of kindness and hospitality at the hands of men who before my election had been strangers to me in all but name."[27]

On joining the Sette, a new member was required to assume a title reflective of his profession or hobbies, and Symons chose to be known as Brother Speculator. He subsequently explained his choice as being due not so much to his interest in games of chance, but rather to his early realization that "We are engaged, willy-nilly, in the risk of existence, and set in a gamble we cannot evade."[28]

Newly elected members, in accordance with Rule 7, were also expected to read a paper to the Sette within a reasonable period after election, and at the 418th meeting of the Sette on November 23, 1926, Symons spoke on Frederick Baron Corvo, as the late Victorian author Frederick Rolfe (1860–1913) styled himself. Corvo is best remembered as the author of *Hadrian VII*, a novel about a failed and highly quarrelsome candidate for the priesthood who, after years of penury, is elected Pope, and who sets about reforming both the Catholic Church and global politics before being assassinated. Corvo had himself sought but failed to enter the priesthood, and had quarreled with most of his friends and benefactors. He died in poverty in Venice, leaving a number of unpublished works, including *Nicholas Crabbe* and *The Desire and Pursuit of the Whole,* both also semi-autobiographical novels. Symons had been researching Corvo for some time, had bought Corvo manuscripts from Christopher Millard, and, shortly before he addressed the Sette, had borrowed a suitcase of Corvo's letters and manuscripts from Corvo's literary executor, materials he was subsequently able to purchase together with the copyrights.

Symons's guests for that dinner included C. H. Pirie-Gordon, a one-time friend and collaborator of Rolfe's. Shane Leslie, who had published an article on Corvo in the *London Mercury* in 1923, and who was to be the dedicatee of Symons's *The Quest for Corvo*, attended as the guest of Vyvyan Holland.

The paper was subsequently printed and distributed to members of the Sette, and in addition to the limited edition of 182 copies, an extra-limited edition of 17 copies included a page of Corvo's handwriting as frontispiece. The paper was subsequently published in an amended form in *Life and Letters*.[29] This paper was the precursor to Symons's *The Quest for Corvo*, which was published in 1934.

In 1927, Symons, who had a deep interest in African exploration, delivered a paper on Emin Pasha. As the menu card for that dinner put it, "it is His Oddshippe's intention to allow BROTHER A.J.A. Symons (Speculator) to mislead the company on the subject of EMIN GOVERNOR OF EQUITORIA."[30] *Emin* was published in an attractive limited edition of 300 copies by the Curwen Press in 1928, representing the first use in England of the Lutetia typeface designed by Jan van Krimpen. Symons read a further paper on Edgar Allan Poe at the 439th Meeting in February 1929, which was subsequently published in *Life and Letters*.[31] Symons delivered "An Episode in the Life of the Queen of Sheba" at a Ladies' Night held by the Sette on June 25, 1929 (443rd Meeting). This was subsequently published privately by Symons and Albert Ehrman, owner of the Broxbourne Library of incunabula and early printed books, in an edition of 150 copies, and again in the October 1930 edition of *Farrago*. It was Symons's only attempt at fiction.

Symons was an active participant in the Sette, being one of only three members to attend all eight meetings in 1926–27 and one of only five members to attend all nine meetings in 1928–29, according to the respective Year-Bokes for the Sette. Unfortunately, a Year-Boke was not issued by the Sette for either 1929–30, the year in which Symons served as Secretary, and of which he would consequently have been the author, or 1938–39, the year that Symons served as President.

Symons was a dedicated signer of his own books, and his calligraphic inscriptions enhance many volumes. In 1936, Percy Smith, the artist and typographer, included a letter from Symons in his *Lettering: A Handbook of Modern Alphabets*, noting that the letter reproduced represented Symons's normal handwriting, used for at least 15 years.[32] Symons particularly enjoyed devising new versions of his signature, and some of his letters include remarkable examples. Symons was also a talented amateur forger, and both Julian Symons[33] and Percy Muir[34] related several occasions on which Symons executed forgeries to demonstrate his capabilities.

Symons was also attracted to bookplates and had a series of six, as well as an earlier rubber stamp. While five of the bookplates recorded his ownership with various levels of decoration, one was designed by Valentin Le Campion, the Russian-born wood-engraver whose work was exhibited at The First Edition Club, and depicts a man raising his glass at a convivial dinner. The December 1935 edition of *The Studio* includes "Ex Libris: The Mark of Possession," an article by Symons on bookplates, which he describes as "fascinating personal expressions of the love of books."[35]

The Club held several exhibitions of bookbindings, including bindings by Sybil Pye and Frieda Thiersch. Commencing in 1934, Symons had 25[36] copies of a number of trade books bound in special bindings by Henry Wood, a leading bindery, for sale to members of the Club's Binding Group, including *The Poetical Works of Ernest Dowson* edited by Desmond Flower, *Farmer's Glory* by A. G. Street with wood engravings by Gwen Raverat, and *The Works of Shelley*. In 1929, Symons acquired the complete printing of *Across the Threshold* by Charles Ricketts (as Paul Raymond), which had been printed at the Curwen Press with a distinctive Ricketts-designed binding, for sale to the Club's members. In the same year, Symons was included in the lecture series *Tradition and Experiment* at the City Literary Institute. The title of Symons's lecture was "Tradition in Biography," but he used the opportunity to express his views on the inadequacies of most biographies, while praising Lytton Strachey for his innovations; other lecturers in the series included Edmund Blunden, T. S. Eliot, Edith Sitwell, and Rebecca West.

The year 1929 also saw the first Corvine Banquet, purportedly organized by the mysterious, anonymous Grand Master but actually organized by Symons and financed by J. Maundy-Gregory, a collector of Corvo. The dinner was held on June 27 at the Ambassador Club, then owned by Maundy-Gregory, and Corvo manuscripts and the Borgia genealogical scroll (the "Borgiata") prepared by Corvo himself were displayed. The 17 guests included R. M. Dawkins, Sholto Douglas, Harry Pirie-Gordon, and Grant Richards, friends and collaborators of Corvo, as well as friends from The First Edition Club and the Sette such as Vyvyan Holland, Ivor Stewart-Liberty, and Ralph Straus. Corvo's *The Bull Against the Enemy of the Anglican Race,* a violent attack on Lord Northcliffe[37] written in the form of a papal bull issued by the fictitious Pope Hadrian VII, was printed for Symons in an edition of 50 copies for distribution to attendees, and the proceedings, and attendees, were recorded in *A True Recital of the Procedure of the First Banquet held by the Corvine Society.*[38]

James Laver has provided a detailed description of the evening in his autobiography, *Museum Piece,* and states that the eight-course dinner was one of the most remarkable meals he had ever eaten, and of almost unbelievable lavishness.[39] Shane Leslie, R. M. Dawkins, Grant Richards, Sholto Douglas, and Symons all made speeches, and numerous toasts were drunk. *A True Recital* includes a footnote by Symons to the effect that "One final toast to the Baron was drunk in Corvo Gran Spumante, and then the meeting did not so much end as deliquesce."[40]

A second Corvine Banquet was held in October of the same year, this time with 30 attendees, and a similar commemorative record was produced.

In 1930, Symons took the lease on Brick House, a delightful Georgian village house on the village green in Finchingfield, Essex, for £60 a year and henceforth largely spent his weekends there. Symons furnished Brick House with a substantial collection of Victoriana, including musical boxes. Brick House was to become his home after the commencement of World War Two and the repository of both his library and the possessions of Vyvyan Holland, as well as the publications and library of The First Edition Club and the publications of the Wine and Food Society.

Membership of the Sette led to further significant friendships for Symons, including with Maurice Healy, King's Counsel and oenophile, and through Healy with André Simon, the celebrated epicure. In 1931, Symons, Simon, and Healy founded the Saintsbury Club, another London dining club, with Simon as President and Symons as Secretary. The Saintsbury Club was formed to honor Professor George Saintsbury, a leading literary scholar and, more importantly for the co-founders, author in 1920 of *Notes on a Cellar-Book*. Ironically, even though the founders offered to hold a lunch in his honor in Bath where he then lived, Saintsbury declined to participate. Not at all daunted, the founders of the club designated Saintsbury as President of the club and, following his death, as perpetual President.

The Saintsbury Club, which was limited to 50 members and initially held semi-annual meetings, continues to this day. Initial members included Vyvyan Holland and Dr. Williamson, as well as Duff Cooper and Compton Mackenzie. In 1943, André Simon published *The Saintsbury Club: A Scrap Book*,[41] which documented the club's first 12 years and which includes the elaborate menus for each meeting. A further history of the Saintsbury Club was provided by Vyvyan Holland in his *Drink and Be Merry*.[42] Speeches ("Orations") were made at these meetings, and were themselves often printed and distributed to members.

Increasing financial pressures compelled Symons to attempt the sale in 1932 of his "nineties" collection of books and manuscripts through Percy Muir of Elkin Mathews. The catalogue (no. 42) issued by Elkin Mathews, entitled *Books of the Nineties*, included large numbers of Beardsley, Corvo, Moore, and Wilde items. Market conditions, however, resulted in only about a third in value of the collection being sold. In his three-part article in *The Book Collector*, Percy Muir has described the extraordinarily complicated financial background to this sale, which resulted from Symons's own byzantine financial dealings. As Muir put it, "It had become the rule of his life to be in debt, to live on money that he owed and had no prospect of repaying; to pledge every asset tangible, contingent, or imaginary, and immediately to repledge it . . . if the opportunity occurred."[43]

In 1933, Duckworth published Symons's biography *H. M. Stanley* in its Great Lives Series, and in 1934 Symons contributed *A Bibliographical Check-list of Baron Corvo* to Percy Muir's *Points: Second Series*

1866–1934.[44] In 1934, *The Quest for Corvo: An Experiment in Biography* appeared and was an immediate success, going into three impressions, and then appearing as a Penguin paperback, of which 170,000 copies were printed within ten years.[45]

The Quest for Corvo was groundbreaking in its combination of the biographical facts about the subject with details of the biographer's pursuit of those facts, and was favorably reviewed by James Agate, David Garnett, Graham Greene, Desmond MacCarthy, and Harold Nicolson, among others. Percy Muir memorably described it as "so much better than anything Corvo himself wrote."[46] *The Quest* records the steps that Symons took to communicate with Corvo's brother Herbert (1862–1932), who did not wish a biography to be written of his brother, and a series of people who befriended Corvo, as well as to find Corvo's missing manuscripts. In particular, *The Quest* describes Symons's relationship with Maundy-Gregory, and Maundy-Gregory's success in tracking down missing Corvo material, including the finding of the remaining five copies of *Don Renato: An Ideal Content* in a "rat-infested cellar."[47] It is notable that Symons does not disclose Maundy-Gregory's role in the earlier Corvine Banquets. During the course of his researches, Symons located previously lost manuscripts of Corvo, and subsequently provided introductions to *The Desire and Pursuit of the Whole* (1934) and to *Hubert's Arthur* (1935).[48]

Symons and his wife were by now living increasingly separate lives, with Symons pursuing his myriad interests in London during the week, dining out almost every evening, sleeping at Mount Lebanon and only spending weekends in Finchingfield, where his wife lived full-time. Symons commenced an affair, and in 1936 Symons and his wife were divorced. Gladys Symons went on to marry Frank G. Nutt, another book collector and an original 1922 Committee member of The First Edition Club who was one of the lenders to the First Loan Exhibition. Symons's own affair ended, and he thereafter lived alone.

In 1933, The First Edition Club had held an exhibition of the work of the Nonesuch Press entitled *The First Decade of Work from the Nonesuch Press*. In 1934, a checklist with descriptions of the first 94 Nonesuch publications by Symons and Flower and notes by Franci

Meynell was published in Numbers XIII and XIV of *The Book-Collector's Quarterly.* In 1936, Meynell, Symons, and Flower were co-authors of *The Nonesuch Century*, a sumptuous survey of the first 100 publications from Meynell's Nonesuch Press, with an "Appraisal" of the press by Symons. Symons inscribed copies to Lord Esher, Vyvyan Holland, and André Simon.

The success of the Saintsbury Club inspired Simon and Symons to form the Wine and Food Society (later renamed the International Wine and Food Society) in 1933, again with Simon as President and Symons as Secretary. The object of the Society was to bring together persons with an appreciation of good food and wine in an effort to raise the standard of eating and drinking in Britain. This was to be effected, in part, by organizing "luncheons, tastings and dinners." The Society was based at 6 Little Russell Street alongside The First Edition Club and then the Sette, each with its own letterhead.

The Society was an immediate success and rapidly increased its membership, which grew to 230 members within a month, to 500 within three months, and to 1,000 within a year. Its third meeting, attended by 354 members and guests,[49] was a dinner at the Savoy Hotel to which, according to André Simon in his autobiography *In the Twilight*, Symons invited some of his friends from the press who the next day provided extensive free publicity.[50] By its 49th meeting (its fourth birthday dinner) held at the Langham Hotel, it was necessary to repeat the dinner on three subsequent evenings to accommodate all of the participating members. The 79th meeting was "An Escoffier Dinner" and was held at the Ritz Hotel over three separate evenings in 1939. In 1934, Simon launched chapters of the Society in America, and the Society continues to operate globally.

In 1934, the Society launched the quarterly journal *Wine and Food* with production and advertising under Symons's direction. Symons contributed reports of the Society's activities, reports of memorable meals, book reviews, and two articles: "Walking in Wessex" (issue no. 14), a description of a walking tour with friends through Wiltshire and Dorset, and "When Club Meets Club" (issue no. 19), describing a meeting in Paris of the Saintsbury Club with the Club des Cent, a

French gastronomic club. Issue no. 6 contains an advertisement for Curtis Moffat Photography, while issues no. 13 and 18 contain advertisements for Cartier, all in Symons's calligraphic hand.

Around 1936, Symons, who claimed familiarity with 150 restaurants in London, mused about writing a guide to London's restaurants. The guide was not written but, in 1937, Symons became a contributor to Graham Greene's short-lived magazine *Night and Day*, contributing articles on where to find oysters, Spanish restaurants, and Swiss and German restaurants in London.[51]

Symons continued to run The First Edition Club, and also served as Vice President of the Sette in 1934 and then as President in 1938, but the Wine and Food Society was to dominate Symons's activities for the remainder of the thirties, and to provide the bulk of his income. The outbreak of World War Two, and the consequent introduction of food rationing in Great Britain, instigated the publishing of *The Unration Book Which has Nothing Whatever to do with any Government, and is Based Solely on Common Sense*[52] by the Society, a spoof on the official ration books; Symons had thought that up to one million copies might be sold, but it was not a success, and large numbers had to be pulped.

The war had substantially curtailed the activities of the Wine and Food Society, and consequently Symons's income. Simon, who had assumed Symons's duties, chafed under the burden and under a misapprehension as to the seriousness of Symons's condition, resulting in an acrimonious correspondence between them.[53] This relationship was soon mended.

Symons again decided to sell a portion of his library, and a catalogue entitled *The Library of a Collector and a Man of Letters* was issued by Elkin Mathews. This time, according to Muir,[54] the catalogue was successful. In addition, Francis Meynell organized a subscription to benefit Symons, much as Symons himself had organized a subscription for Vincent O'Sullivan (1868–1940), the nineties poet and writer.

In November 1939, before the catalogue was issued, Symons was stricken by the illness which was to kill him in August 1941, and which was ultimately found to be a hemorrhage into his brain stem. After recovering somewhat at his mother's house, Mount Lebanon, he retreated to Finchingfield. Francis Meynell noted that he "had never known a man so heroic in disaster."[55]

During this period, Symons completed a chapter on Theodore Hook for inclusion in *English Wits: Their Lives and Jests*, edited by Leonard Russell,[56] and, returning to the theme of African exploration, started work on a life of Captain Stokes and a study of the explorations of Richard Burton and John Speke. He also started a history of the Tennants of Glenconner, a family of Scottish industrialists. None was completed. He continued to maintain an extensive correspondence, including with C. K. Ogden, the philosopher and proponent of Basic English, and also a collector of musical boxes, including some sold to him by Symons, and Edward Bawden, an artist who lived near Finchingfield and on whom Symons had contributed an article to *Art and Industry* in 1937.[57]

On August 26, 1941, Symons died in Colchester Hospital, and was buried in the parish churchyard of Finchingfield, where his grave monument bears his self-written epitaph "AJAS ALAS." The *Times* carried his obituary.[58] Vyvyan Holland and Julian Symons wrote memorial essays for *Horizon*,[59] and notices appeared in *Wine and Food*, including by Sir Francis Colchester-Wemyss, Desmond Flower, Doris Langley Moore, Percy Muir, and André Simon.[60]

Despite his considerable achievements, Symons's reputation was controversial. Percy Muir's opinion of Symons has previously been noted. Julian Symons noted that visitors to The First Edition Club had a "nebulous feeling that they were in the presence of a literary adventurer whose suggestions should be examined with some care."[61] Osbert Burdett, author of *The Beardsley Period,* on which he had been helped by Symons, wrote to Symons that he had a friend who thought Symons was "accustomed to regard people as clay to be shapen to a vessel of your own design."[62]

Percy Muir considered Symons's *A Bibliography of the First Editions of Books by William Butler Yeats* to be "a typical example of his ability to skim the surface of a subject without penetrating it." Muir also recorded Symons's "boasting admission that money was the only thing that really interested him."[63] Hugh Walpole, who bought Corvo material from Symons, wrote that he could not abide Symons, and Stanley Morison deemed Symons to be an "unadmirable man."[64]

Following his death, Symons's library was dispersed, with a portion being auctioned through Sotheby's in 194 lots (one lot alone included 170 volumes on African travel and exploration). In 1943, his best musical boxes went to the Pitt-Rivers Museum in Oxford, and his furniture and remaining 65 musical boxes went to auction.

Symons was not, however, forgotten. Julian Symons published an article about him ("A Player of Games") and another about Corvo in *The Saturday Book*, before writing *A.J.A. Symons: His Life and Speculations* in 1950 and contributing an introduction to a new edition of *The Quest for Corvo* in 1955. That edition also reprints the two Proceedings of The Corvine Banquets and Corvo's *Bull Against the Enemy of the Anglican Race*. Julian also edited *Essays and Biographies*, a collection of some of Symons's unpublished and limited distribution pieces, in 1969, and in 1985 read "A.J.A. Symons: Brother Speculator" to members of the Double Crown Club in London. Julian also edited *A.J.A. Symons to Wyndham Lewis: Twenty-Four Letters* in 1982 and *Two Brothers: Fragments of a Correspondence* in 1985, both published by the Tragara Press. Julian refers to his brother in other works, particularly *Julian Symons: A Bibliography*.[65]

Percy Muir published a three-part essay on Symons under the title "Bibliomanes I: A.J.A. Symons" in *The Book Collector*, and described his relationship with Symons in *Minding My Own Business,* his autobiography. Muir also described Symons's book dealings with Hugh Walpole in "Bibliomanes II: Hugh Walpole." Muir liked Symons but disapproved of his book dealing methods, and was careful never to advance him money.[66]

George F. Sims, who developed a relationship with Julian Symons, and through him with Symons's mother and with his ex-wife, offered numerous Symons items through many of his 107 catalogues, including Catalogue No. 2, which included a group of Corvo's letters, Catalogue No. 3, which included a collection of Wildeana, and *A Catalogue of Letters, Manuscript Papers and Books of Frederick Rolfe (Baron Corvo)*, all from Symons's library. The Corvo catalogue was bought in its entirety by David Roth, a Corvo collector, and became part of his Martyr Worthy collection of Corvo, now held in the Rare Book & Manuscript Library of Columbia University. Sims's Catalogue 29 was entitled *Books and Manuscripts Including Some from the Collection of the Late A.J.A. Symons,* and Sims notes that "The majority of the books described herein are from" Symons's collection. Included in Sims's Autumn 1949 catalogue (item 258) was a 380-folio-page calligraphic catalogue of his collection by Symons. Sims went on to write a two-part article on Symons in 1981 for *Antiquarian Book Monthly Review.* This was included in Sims's later *The Rare Book Game.*[67]

In 1991, Stone Trough Books issued a 50th anniversary catalogue entitled *A.J.A. Symons 1900–1941* with commentary from Julian Symons and a photograph of a portrait of Symons by Natalie Sieveking. Symons was the subject of a BBC television profile in November 1993, presented by Julian Symons in its *Bookends* series. In 2013, a third Corvine Banquet was held by a group of Corvo enthusiasts, and a third commemorative pamphlet was issued. In 2014, *The Corvo Cult: History of an Obsession* by Robert Scoble was published, containing much useful biographical information on Symons, who also appears on its cover. [68] In 2016, a new edition of *The Quest for Corvo* was published by the Tartarus Press with an introductory essay by Mark Valentin and photographs of Symons and some of Symons's research materials, including items from the Donald Weeks collection at Leeds University. This edition also includes Symons's essay "Tradition in Biography" from *Tradition and Experiment in Present-day Literature.*[69]

There are significant holdings of Symons material in the British Library, the William Andrew Clark Memorial Library at the UCLA Library, the Rare Books & Manuscripts Library of Columbia University, Rare and Manuscript Collections – Cornell University, the Berg Collection at the New York Public Library, Special Collections at the University of Delaware Library, Special Collections at Leeds University Library, Rare Books and Special Collections at Princeton University Library, and the Harry Ransom Center, the University of Texas at Austin.

NOTES

1 Desmond Flower, *Fellows in Foolscap: Memoirs of a Publisher* (London: Rober Hale, 1991), 79.

2 Julian Symons, *A.J.A. Symons: His Life and Speculations* (London: Eyre & Spot tiswoode, 1950), 268.

3 Letter from A.J.A. Symons to Victoria Emily ("Gladys") Weeks, no date pro vided, quoted in ibid., 33.

4 Julian Symons, *A.J.A. Symons: His Life*, 27.

5 Percy Muir, "Bibliomanes I: A.J.A. Symons, Part 1," *The Book Collector* 3, no. II (Autumn 1954): 199.

6 Ibid., 200.

7 Flower, *Fellows in Foolscap*, 80.

8 James Laver, *Museum Piece* (Boston: Houghton Mifflin, 1964), 165.

9 A.J.A. Symons, "The Book-Collector's Apology," *The Book-Collector's Quarterly* no. I (December 1930): 48.

10 Julian Symons, *A.J.A. Symons: His Life*, 25.

11 Menu card in Symons papers held by Special Collections at the University o Delaware Library.

12 Julian Symons, *A.J.A. Symons: His Life*, 39.

13 List of Members of The First Edition Club, 1929.

14 A.J.A. Symons, "Book Collectors' Notes," *The Spectator*, April 5, 1924, 12.

15 A.J.A. Symons, "The Work of the First Edition Club," *Penrose's Annual* 31 (1929): 25

16 Menu card in A.J.A. Symons Papers held by Special Collections at the University of Delaware Library.

17 Shane Leslie, introduction to *The Quest for Corvo* by A.J.A. Symons (London Folio Society, 1952), xvii.

18 Letter from A.J.A. Symons to Leon D. Becker, 9 March 1931.

19 Financial information derived from Chapters 6 and 7 of Julian Symons, *A.J.A Symons: His Life*.

20 First Edition Club Notes, *The Book-Collector's Quarterly*, no. II, March 1931, 114.

21 Julian Symons, *A.J.A. Symons: His Life*, 55.

22 Julian Symons, *Oscar Wilde: A Problem in Biography* (Yellow Barn Press, 1988), 17.

23 *Books and Manuscripts Including Some from the Collection of the Late A.J.A. Symons* Catalogue 29 issued by G. F. Sims (Rare Books), n.d., item 70.

24 *Long Shadows: Memoirs of Shane Leslie* (London: John Murray, 1966), 250.

25 Invitation Card to attend the 430th Meeting of Ye Sette of Odd Volumes, 28th February 1928.

26 *Booklet of The Sette of Odd Volumes* (November 1938): 15.

27 *Inaugural Address of His Oddshippe Bro. A.J.A. Symons delivered to the Sette of Odd Volumes* (London: Curwen Press, 1938), 3.

28 Ibid.

29 A.J.A. Symons, "Frederick Baron Corvo," *Life and Letters* 1, no. 2 (July 1928): 81–101

0 Menu card for the 428th Meeting of the Sette held on 23rd November 1927.

1 A.J.A. Symons, "Edgar Allen Poe," *Life and Letters* 2, no. 10 (March 1929): 163–178.

2 Percy Smith, *Lettering: A Handbook of Modern Alphabets* (London: A. & C. Black Ltd., 1936), 57.

3 Julian Symons, *A.J.A. Symons: His Life*, 58.

4 Muir, "Bibliomanes I: A.J.A. Symons, Part 1," 208–10.

5 A.J.A. Symons, "Ex Libris: The Mark of Possession," *The Studio*, Books and Book Plates Number (December 1935): 316.

6 Flower, *Fellows in Foolscap*, 81.

7 Cecil Woolf, *A Bibliography of Frederick Rolfe: Baron Corvo, the Soho Bibliographies* (London: Rupert Hart-Davis, 1957), 57.

8 A.J.A. Symons, *A True Recital of the Procedure of the First Banquet held by the Corvine Society, June 27th, 1929 at the Ambassador Club*.

9 Laver, *Museum Piece*, 166.

0 A.J.A. Symons, *A True Recital*, 19.

1 *The Saintsbury Club: A Scrap Book by "The Cellarer"* [André L. Simon] (London: Privately printed for the Saintsbury Club, 1943).

2 Vyvyan Holland, *Drink and Be Merry* (London: Victor Gollancz, 1967).

3 Percy Muir, "Bibliomanes I: A.J.A. Symons, Part 2," *The Book Collector*, Winter 1954, 250.

4 A.J.A. Symons, *H. M. Stanley* (London: Duckworth, 1933); "A Bibliographical Check-list of Baron Corvo" in Percy Muir, *Points: Second Series 1866–1934* (London: Constable, 1934).

5 Robert Scoble, *The Corvo Cult* (London: Strange Attractor Press, 2014), 315.

6 Percy Muir, "Bibliomanes I: A.J.A. Symons, Part 3," *The Book Collector*, Summer 1955, 130.

7 A.J.A. Symons, *The Quest for Corvo* [245].

8 Frederick Rolfe Baron Corvo, *The Desire and Pursuit of the Whole: A Romance of Modern Venice* (London: Cassell, 1934); *Hubert's Arthur, Being Certain Curious Documents Found Among the Literary Remains of Mr. N.C., Here Produced by Prospero and Caliban* (London: Cassell, 1935).

9 *Wine and Food* 1, Spring Number (1934): 68.

0 André L. Simon, *In the Twilight* (London: Michael Joseph, 1969), 55.

1 Graham Greene, *Night and Day* (London: Chatto & Windus, 1985), 132, 203, and 263, respectively.

2 A.L.S./AJAS [André L. Simon and A.J.A. Symons], *The Unration Book* (London: The Wine and Food Society, 1939).

3 Julian Symons, *A.J.A. Symons: His Life*, 232.

4 Muir, "Bibliomanes I: A.J.A. Symons, Part 3," 127.

5 Francis Meynell, *My Lives* (New York: Random House, 1971), 183.

6 A.J.A. Symons, "Theodore Hook," in *English Wits: Their Lives and Jests*, ed. Leonard Russell (London: Hutchinson, 1940).

57 A.J.A. Symons, "Edward Bawden – The Work of a Designer and Illustrato Whose Name Is Becoming Increasingly Familiar," *Art and Industry* 22, April 193 (London: The Studio, 1937).

58 *The Times*, London, August 29, 1941.

59 Julian Symons, "Memoir of A.J.A. Symons," and Vyvyan Holland, "Memoir o A.J.A. Symons," *Horizon* 4(22), October 1941.

60 *Wine and Food*, no. 31, Autumn 1941 (André Simon); *Wine and Food*, no. 32, Winte 1941 (Trevor Blakemore, Sir Frederick Colchester-Wemyss, and P. H. Muir); *Win and Food*, no. 35, Autumn 1942 (Desmond Flower and Doris Langley Moore).

61 Julian Symons, *A.J.A. Symons: His Life*, 60.

62 Osbert Burdett, *The Beardsley Period: An Essay in Perspective* (London: The Bodle Head, 1925); *A.J.A. Symons: His Life*, 60, includes quotation from letter from Os bert Burdett to A.J.A. Symons, no date provided.

63 A.J.A. Symons, *A Bibliography of First Editions of Books by William Butler Yeat* (London: The First Edition Club, 1924); Muir, "Bibliomanes I: A.J.A. Symons Part 3," 130; "Bibliomanes I: A.J.A. Symons, Part 2," 291.

64 Scoble, *The Corvo Cult*, 266; letter from Stanley Morison to Oliver Simon, 1954 quoted in Nicolas Barker, *Stanley Morison* (London: Macmillan, 1972), 449.

65 Julian Symons, "A Player of Games," *The Saturday Book 4*, ed. Leonard Russel (London: Hutchinson, 1944); "The Battle for Holywell: A Story of Baron Corvo, *The Saturday Book 5*, ed. Leonard Russell (London: Hutchinson, 1945); introduc tion to A.J.A. Symons, *The Quest for Corvo: An Experiment in Biography* (London Cassell, 1955); A.J.A. Symons, *Essays and Biographies*, ed. Julian Symons (London Cassell, 1969); *A.J.A. Symons to Wyndham Lewis: Twenty-Four Letters*, with com ments by Julian Symons (Edinburgh: Tragara Press, 1982); Julian Symons, ed., *Tw Brothers: Fragments of a Correspondence* (Edinburgh: Tragara Press, 1985); John Walsdorf and Bonnie J. Allen, *Julian Symons: A Bibliography with Commentarie and a Personal Memoir by Julian Symons and a Preface by H. R. F. Keating* (New Castle, DE: Oak Knoll Press; Winchester: St. Paul's Bibliographies, 1996).

66 Percy Muir, "Bibliomanes I: A.J.A. Symons," *The Book Collector* 3, no. 3 (Autumn 1954); 3, no. 4 (Winter 1954); 4, no. 2 (Summer 1955); *Minding My Own Busines* (London: Chatto & Windus, 1956); "Bibliomanes II: Hugh Walpole, Part 1," *Th Book Collector* 4, no. 3 (Autumn 1955), "Bibliomanes II: Hugh Walpole, Part 2," *Th Book Collector* 4, no. 4 (Winter 1955); "Bibliomanes I," 200.

67 George Sims, "A.J.A. Symons Part I: The First Edition Club," *Antiquarian Boo Monthly Review* 8, no. 10, issue 90 (October 1981) and "A.J.A. Symons Part II: Th First Edition Club," *Antiquarian Book Monthly Review* 8, no. 11, issue 91 (Novem ber 1981); *The Rare Book Game* (Philadelphia: Holmes Publishing, 1994).

68 Robert Scoble, *The Corvo Cult*.

69 A.J.A. Symons, "Tradition in Biography," *Tradition and Experiment in Present day Literature* (London: Oxford University Press, 1929) with a preface by J. G Williams.

II

SYMONS'S PUBLISHED WORKS
A PRELIMINARY LIST

1922

A Bibliographical Catalogue of the First Loan Exhibition of Books and Manuscripts Held by The First Edition Club

A.J.A. Symons
The First Edition Club. Curwen Press. Quarter canvas with red paper labels
Limited to 500 copies

1924

A Bibliography of the First Editions of Books by William Butler Yeats

Compiled with a Preface by A.J.A. Symons
The First Edition Club. Curwen Press. Boards with paper label
Limited to 500 copies

Book Collectors' Notes

The Spectator
Series of six articles by Symons in April–September

1925

A Bibliography of the First Editions Proof Copies and Manuscripts of Books by Lord Byron exhibited at The Fourth Exhibition held by The First Edition Club January 1925

Compiled with a preface by A.J.A. Symons
The First Edition Club. Curwen Press. Black buckram
Limited to 500 copies

Ten Tales

Ambrose Bierce
Introduction by A.J.A. Symons
The First Edition Club. Curwen Press. Red cloth
Limited to 500 copies

1927

Baron Corvo

A.J.A. Symons
The Curwen Press. Privately printed opuscula of the Sette of Odd Volumes, Number 81. Paper covers
Limited to 199 copies of which 17 copies were printed on hand-made paper, were bound in blue morocco, and included a page of Corvo's handwriting a frontispiece

1928

Life and Letters, Vol. 1, No. 2, July 1928

Journal
Includes "Frederick Baron Corvo" by Symons
Curwen Press. Quarter buckram with decorated boards
Limited to 200 copies
There was also an ordinary edition in paper covers

An Anthology of "Nineties" Verse

Edited with an introduction by A.J.A. Symons
Elkins Mathews & Marrot, Ltd. Boards with illustrated dust jacket

Emin: The Governor of Equitoria

A.J.A. Symons
The Fleuron. Curwen Press. Quarter buckram with patterned paper on boards
Limited to 300 copies

1929

Life and Letters, Vol. 2, No. 10, March 1929

Journal
Includes "Edgar Allen Poe" by Symons

An Episode in the Life of the Queen of Sheba

A.J.A. Symons
Privately printed for Albert Ehrman and A.J.A. Symons. Curwen-patterned wrapper
Limited to 150 copies

Tradition and Experiment in Present-day Literature: Essays
Oxford University Press. Green cloth with dust jacket
Includes "Tradition in Biography" by Symons

Penrose's Annual, Vol. 31
Percy Lund Humphreys & Co. Ltd. Cloth
Includes "The Work of The First Edition Club" by Symons

A True Recital of the Procedure of the first Banquet held by
the CORVINE SOCIETY
A.J.A. Symons
[Curwen Press]. Pamphlet.

A True Recital of the Procedure of the second Banquet held by
the CORVINE SOCIETY
A.J.A. Symons
[Curwen Press]. Pamphlet.

1930

The Fleuron: A Journal of Typography, No. 7
Journal
Includes "An Unacknowledged Movement in Fine Printing: The Ty-
pography of the Eighteen-Nineties" by Symons

The Book-Collector's Quarterly, No. I
Edited by Desmond Flower and A.J.A. Symons
Cassell & Co. Red buckram
Includes "The Book Collector's Apology" by Symons
Limited to 100 copies
There was also an ordinary edition

Penrose's Annual, Vol. 32
Percy Lund Humphreys & Co. Ltd. Quarter cloth
Includes "The English and American Books of 1928" by Symons

Farrago, Number Three, October 1930
Simon Nowell-Smith. Wrapper
Includes "An Episode in the Life of the Queen of Sheba" by Symons

1931

The Book-Collector's Quarterly, No. III

Edited by Desmond Flower and A.J.A. Symons
Cassell & Co. Red buckram
Includes "Point Counter-Point" by Symons
Limited to 100 copies
There was also an ordinary edition

1932

The Book-Collector's Quarterly, No. V

Edited by Desmond Flower and A.J.A. Symons
Cassell & Co. Patterned cloth
Includes "Edition and Impression" by Symons
Limited to 100 copies
There was also an ordinary edition

The Book-Collector's Quarterly, No. VIII

Edited by Desmond Flower and A.J.A. Symons
Cassell & Co. Patterned cloth
Includes "On Selecting the Fifty Books of the Year" by Symons
Limited to 75 copies
There was also an ordinary edition

1933

H. M. Stanley

A.J.A. Symons
Duckworth. Red cloth with dust jacket

1934

The Quest for Corvo: An Experiment in Biography

A.J.A. Symons
Cassell & Co. Black cloth with dust jacket

The Desire and Pursuit of the Whole

Frederick Rolfe Baron Corvo
Introduction by A.J.A. Symons
Cassell. Green cloth with dust jacket

Points, Second Series, 1866–1934
>   Percy H. Muir
>   *Bibliographia: Studies in Book History and Book Structure*
>   Constable. Quarter parchment on marbled boards with glassine wrapper
>   Includes "A Bibliographical Check-list of Baron Corvo" by Symons

The Book-Collector's Quarterly, No. XIII
>   Edited by Desmond Flower and A.J.A. Symons
>   Cassell & Co. Patterned cloth
>   Includes "Post-War English Bookbinding: An Address to Members of
>   The First Edition Club" and "Modern English Bookbindings at The
>   First Edition Club Reviewed," both by Symons

The Book-Collector's Quarterly, No. XV
>   Edited by Desmond Flower and A.J.A. Symons
>   Cassell & Co. Wrappers
>   Includes "The Nineteenth Century Forgeries" and "Notes on the Fifty
>   Books of the Year" by Symons

Is It Wise?
>   A.J.A. Symons
>   Wests, Steyning. Leaflet
>   *Limited to 25 copies*
>   *Included in the series "Weppons of Peace" issued by Philip Gosse*

1935

Hubert's Arthur. Being Certain Curious Documents Found Among the Literary Remains of Mr. N.C., Here Produced by Prospero and Caliban
>   Frederick Rolfe Baron Corvo
>   Introduction by A.J.A. Symons
>   Cassell. Green cloth with dust jacket

Curwen Press News Letter, No. 8, 1934
>   Curwen Press. Journal
>   Includes "Curwen Press Books" by Symons

The Studio, December 1935

Magazine
Includes "Ex Libris: The Mark of Possession" and "Book Design This Year: Illustration – Typography – Binding" by Symons

1936

Fords and Bridges, Vol. 1, Part 4, February 1936

Journal
Includes "A Forgotten Dinner Party" by Symons

The Nonesuch Century

A.J.A. Symons, Francis Meynell, and Desmond Flower
Nonesuch Press. Green buckram
Limited to 750 copies

The Epicure's Anthology of Banqueting Delights

The Golden Cockerell Press. Leather label on boards.
Includes "The Epicure and the Epicurean" by Symons
Limited to 150 copies
There was also an ordinary edition in pink cloth with dust jacket

1937

Twentieth Century Verse, Vol. 6/7, November/December 1937

Wyndham Lewis Double Number
Journal
Includes [Wyndham Lewis] "The Novelist" by Symons

Art and Industry, Vol. 22, No. 90 (April 1937)

Magazine
Includes "Edward Bawden – The Work of a Designer and Illustrator Whose Name Is Becoming Increasingly Familiar" by Symons

Night and Day

Edited by Graham Greene
Magazine
Symons contributed the "Round the Restaurants" column for September 16 ("Where to Eat Oysters"), October 23 ("Spanish Restaurants"), and December 16 ("Swiss and German Restaurants")

1938

Wine and Food, No. 14
Journal
Includes "Walking in Wessex" by Symons

Wine and Food, No. 19
Journal
Includes "When Club Meets Club" by Symons

Practical Planning with Books
National Book Council. Pamphlet
Includes "First Editions" by Symons

Penrose's Annual, Vol. 40
Percy Lund Humphreys & Co. Ltd. Cloth
Includes "The Detection of a Bibliographic Forgery" by Symons

Inaugural Address of His Oddshippe Br. A.J.A. Symons
(Speculator)
The Sette of Odd Volumes
The Curwen Press. Pamphlet

1939

The Unration Book
ALS/AJAS [André L. Simon/ A.J.A. Symons]
Wine and Food Society. Pamphlet

1940

English Wits: Their Lives and Jests
Edited by Leonard Russell
Hutchinson. Cloth with dust jacket
Includes "Theodore Hook" by Symons

1941

Horizon, Vol. 3, No. 16, April 1941
Journal
Includes "Wilde at Oxford" by Symons

Horizon, Vol. 4, No. 22, October 1941
>Journal
>Includes "The Diner-out" by Symons
>Originally published in *Fords and Bridges* in 1936

1945

Horizon, Vol. 12, No. 71, November 1945
>Journal
>Includes "Irving and the Irvingites" by Symons

1952

The Quest for Corvo: An Experiment in Biography
>A.J.A. Symons
>Introductions by Sir Norman Birkett and Shane Leslie
>The Folio Society. Quarter buckram

1955

The Quest for Corvo: An Experiment in Biography
>A.J.A. Symons
>Introduction by Julian Symons
>Cassell. Cloth with dust jacket

1969

Essays and Biographies
>A.J.A. Symons
>Edited by Julian Symons
>Cassell. Blue cloth with dust jacket

1979

Is It Wise?
>A.J.A. Symons
>Fonthill Press. Leaflet
>*Limited to about 125 copies*
>*Originally included in the series "Weppons of Peace" issued by Philip Gosse*
>*in 1934*

1982

A.J.A. Symons to Wyndham Lewis: Twenty-Four Letters

Julian Symons
Tragara Press. Pamphlet
Limited to 120 copies

1985

Two Brothers: Fragments of a Correspondence

Julian Symons
Tragara Press. Pamphlet
Limited to 130 copies

2010

One Lump or Two: Tea, Twinings and Edward Bawden, with Limericks by A.J.A. Symons

Essay by Peyton Skipwith
Mainstone Press. Paperback

III

LIST OF PUBLICATIONS ISSUED
BY THE FIRST EDITION CLUB

1922

1. A Bibliographical Catalogue of the First Loan Exhibition of Books and Manuscripts Held by The First Edition Club 1922

A.J.A. Symons
Curwen Press
Limited to 500 copies

1923

2. A Reply to Z

William Hazlitt
Introduction by Charles Whibley
Curwen Press
Limited to 300 copies

1924

3. A Bibliography of the First Editions of Books by William Butler Yeats

A.J.A. Symons
Curwen Press
Limited to 500 copies

4. Sixty-Three Unpublished Designs

C. Lovat Fraser
Introduction by Holbrook Jackson
Curwen Press
Limited to 500 copies

1925

5. Bibliographical Catalogue of First Editions, Proof Copies and Manuscripts of Books by Lord Byron

A.J.A. Symons

Curwen Press
Limited to 500 copies

6. Ten Tales
Ambrose Bierce
Introduction by A.J.A. Symons
Curwen Press
Limited to 500 copies

7. London Tradesmen's Cards of the XVIIIth Century: An Account of Their Origin and Use
Ambrose Heal
B. T. Batsford
Curwen Press
Limited to 100 copies
Further 950 copies for Batsford

8. Bibliography of the First Editions of Published and Privately Printed Books and Pamphlets by Austin Dobson
Alban Dobson
Curwen Press
Limited to 500 copies

1926

9. Twenty Letters to Conrad
Introduction by G. Jean-Aubry
Curwen Press
Limited to 220 copies

10. Thirty Bindings Selected from The First Edition Club's Seventh Exhibition
G. D. Hobson
Chiswick Press
Limited to 600 copies

11. Gulliver's Travels
Jonathan Swift
Introduction by Harold Williams
Oxford University Press
Limited to 750 copies

1928

12. The Ravenna Journal

Lord Byron
Introduction by Lord Ernle
Curwen Press
Limited to 500 copies

13. A Select Bibliography of the Principal Modern Presses Public and Private in Great Britain and Ireland

G. S. Tomkinson
Introduction by B. H. Newdigate
Curwen Press
Limited to 1,000 copies

14. The Pen and Type-Design

Graily Hewitt
Oxford University Press
Limited to 250 copies

15. Book Clubs and Printing Societies of Great Britain and Ireland (1570-1822)

Harold Williams
Curwen Press
Limited to 750 copies

1930

16. The Book of Signs

Rudolf Koch
Translated by Vyvyan Holland
Wil Gerstung
Limited to 500 copies

17. Battle Sketches

Ambrose Bierce
Introduction by A.J.A. Symons
Shakespeare Head Press
Limited to 350 copies

18. John Bell, 1745-1831: Bookseller, Printer, Publisher, Typographer, Journalist, etc.

Stanley Morison
Cambridge University Press
300 copies printed of which 100 were numbered, bound for, and issued under the imprint of The First Edition Club

1931

19. The English Writing-Masters and Their Copy-Books, 1570-1800: A Biographical Dictionary and a Bibliography

Ambrose Heal
Cambridge University Press
300 copies printed of which 100 were numbered, bound for, and issued under the imprint of The First Edition Club

1932

20. Lettering: A Plea

Percy Smith
Bradley Press
Limited to 400 copies
Further 350 copies for the Dorian Workshop

1933

21. Dreams and Life (Le rève et la vie)

Gérard de Nerval
Translated by Vyvyan Holland
The Boar's Head Press, Manaton, Devon
Limited to 450 copies

1934

22. Maxims of Books and Reading

Holbrook Jackson
Halcyon Press, Maastricht, Holland
Limited to 400 copies

1937

23. The Songs of Meleager Made into English with Designs by Frederick Baron Corvo (Fr. Rolfe) in Collaboration with Sholto Douglas

> Frederick Baron Corvo
> Preface by A.J.A. Symons
> Chiswick Press
> *Limited to 750 copies*

24. Letters from Aubrey Beardsley to Leonard Smithers

> Aubrey Beardsley
> Introduction by R. A. Walker
> Chiswick Press

IV

EXHIBITIONS HELD BY THE FIRST EDITION CLUB

1922

Rare Books, Manuscripts and Bibliographical Curiosities
(The First Loan Exhibition)
First Edition Club Publication No. 1

1924 May

First Editions of the Works of William Butler Yeats
Lent by Sir Lucas King
First Edition Club Publication No. 3

June

The Printed Work of Claude Lovat Fraser
Lent by C. S. Millard
First Edition Club Publication No. 4

1925

First Editions, Proof Copies and Manuscripts of the Works of Lord Byron
Lent by J. Murray
First Edition Club Publication No. 5

1926 May

Eighteenth-Century Tradesmen's cards
Lent by Ambrose Heal
First Edition Club Publication No. 7

May

First Editions, Proof Copies, and Manuscripts by Austin Dobson
First Edition Club Publication No. 8

1927 February

Examples of Fine Book-Bindings of the Sixteenth to Eighteenth Centuries

First Edition Club Publication No. 10

1927 June

Printers' and Typefounders' Specimen Books and Broadsides

No catalogue

1928 May

Selected Examples of Modern English Private Presses

Opened by Sir Frederick Kenyon, KCB
Catalogue not inspected by the author

July

Selected Examples of German Books Privately Printed or Printed by Private Presses

Opened by HE the German Ambassador Herr Friedrich Sthamer
No catalogue

November

First Editions, Proof Copies and Manuscripts of Books by John Galsworthy

No catalogue

1929 March

Presentation and Association Books

No catalogue

One Hundred Czechoslovak Books

April

Bookbindings by Frieda Thiersch

Pamphlet

Fifty Books of the Year 1928

Pamphlet

1930 October
Book-bindings by Sybil Pye
Pamphlet

Books and Manuscripts Relating to the East Indies

Recent French Books

One Hundred Dutch Books
Booklet

Fifty Books of the Year 1929
Catalogue not inspected by the author

1931 January
Manuscripts and Early Printed Books Illustrating "The Art of Good Living" from the Collection of André L. Simon
Pamphlet
Reviewed in *The Book-Collector's Quarterly,* No. II

March
Books, Newspapers, etc. Printed by John Bell ... and by John Browne Bell
Opened by Lord Riddell
Pamphlet

May
Modern Manuscript Books by the Society of Scribes & Illuminators & Others
Opened by Graily Hewitt
Catalogue not inspected by the author. Opening speech reproduced in a leaflet

June
Modern German Bindings
Catalogue not inspected by the author

Fifty Best Books 1930
Pamphlet
Reviewed in *The Book-Collector's Quarterly,* No. I

1931 July

Copy-books by English Writing-Masters from the Collection of Ambrose Heal

First Edition Club Publication No. 19

December

Books Illustrating the Wood-engraving of the Sixties Largely from the Collection of Harold Hartley

1932 February

The Work in Printing and Engraving of Eric Gill

Opened by Eric Gill
Opening speech reproduced in *The Book-Collector's Quarterly*, No. X

April

Chap-Books

June

Books Illustrated by Edy Legrand

Opened by HE the French Ambassador
Pamphlet

July

Fifty Books of the Year 1931

Pamphlet
The Book-Collector's Quarterly, No. III

October

Books and Manuscripts Relative to Buccaneers and Piracy from the Collection of Philip Gosse

Opened by Philip Gosse
Opening speech reproduced in *The Book-Collector's Quarterly*, No. IX

1933 April

Fifty Books of the Year 1932

Opened by Robert Gibbings
Pamphlet

November

The First Decade of Work from the Nonesuch Press

Opened by Francis Meynell
Reviewed in *The Book-Collector's Quarterly,* Nos. XIII-XIV

December

Post-War English Bookbindings

Opened by A.J.A. Symons
Pamphlet
Opening speech reproduced *in The Book-Collector's Quarterly,* No. XIII

1934

Fifty Books of the Year 1933

Pamphlet

1935

Fifty Books 1934

Opened by Walter Runciman, MP and President of the Board of Trade
Pamphlet

The Wood-engravings of Valentin le Campion

Percy Smith's Typographical Work

Opened by Holbrook Jackson
Opening speech reproduced in booklet

1936 June

Fifty Books 1935

Opened by Albert Rutherston
Pamphlet

November

Books Printed in the U.S.S.R. in the Period 1930–1936

Opened by HE the Soviet Ambassador Monsieur Ivan Maisky
Francis Meynell in the Chair
Pamphlet

1937 April

Post-War German Book-Production Including Printing, Calligraphy, Type-Design, Illustration and Trade and Hand-Binding

Opened by Dr. Woermann, Minister Plenipotentiary to the German Embassy

September

The Fifty Books 1936

Opened by Holbrook Jackson
Pamphlet

1938 June

Fifty Books 1937

Opened by Sir Hugh Walpole
Pamphlet

1939 June

Fifty Books 1938

Opened by Shane Leslie
Pamphlet

V

BOOKS RELEVANT TO SYMONS

1921

"Mount Lebanon" 9 Cedars Road, Clapham Common

Contents of the Residence, July 4, 1921
Robinson Fisher & Harding
Auction catalogue

1928

Year-Boke of the Sette of Odd Volumes, No. 34

Ivor Stewart-Liberty, Secretary
The Sette of Odd Volumes. Vellum

1930–35

The Book-Collector's Quarterly, Nos. I-XVII

Edited by Desmond Flower and A.J.A. Symons
Cassell & Co.

1932

Year-Boke of the Sette of Odd Volumes, No. 36

Maurice Healy, Secretary
The Sette of Odd Volumes. Vellum

1934-41

Wine and Food, Nos. 1-30

1936

Lettering: A Handbook of Modern Alphabets

Percy J. Smith
A & C Black. Cloth

1941

Obituary of Symons from *The Times*, August 29, 1941

Horizon, October, Vol. 4, No. 22

Journal

Includes "Memoir of A.J.A. Symons" by Julian Symons and "Memoir of A.J.A. Symons" by Vyvyan Holland

Wine and Food, No. 31

The Wine and Food Society

Includes "A.J.A. Symons, In Memoriam" by André L. Simon

Wine and Food, No. 32

The Wine and Food Society

Includes "In Memoriam: A.J.A. Symons" by Trevor Blakemore, "AYJAY" by P. H. Muir, and "Arising out of No. 31" by Sir Francis Colchester-Wemyss

1942

Wine and Food, No. 35

The Wine and Food Society

Includes "An Empty Glass Turned Down for A.J." by Doris Langley Moore and "AJ" by Desmond Flower

1943

Old English and Modern Furniture, Carpets, A Collection of Musical Boxes and Ivories, English and Continental Wines, Porcelain, Cut Glass, Etc.

The Property of a Lady Removed from Finchingfield, Essex, and Other Private Sources

Knight, Frank & Rutley

Sale catalogue

Catalogue of Printed Books, Including some from the Library of the late A.J.A. Symons: 2 March 1943

Sotheby's

Sale catalogue

1944

The Saturday Book 4

Hutchinson. Red cloth

Includes "A Player of Games" by Julian Symons

1945

The Saturday Book 5

Hutchinson. Red cloth
Includes "The Battle for Holywell: A Story of Baron Corvo" by Julian Symons

1948-1987

Catalogues 1-107

George Sims
G. F. Sims
Book catalogues

1950

A.J.A. Symons: His Life and Speculations

Julian Symons
Eyre & Spottiswoode. Red cloth with pictorial wrappers

1951

The Holbrook Jackson Library: Catalogue 119

Elkin Mathews Ltd. Wrappers

1952

The Quest for Corvo

A.J.A. Symons
Introductory essays by Sir Norman Birkett and Sir Shane Leslie
The Folio Society. Quarter buckram on decorated boards with dust jacket

1954

The Book Collector, Autumn 1954

Journal
Includes "Bibliomanes I: A.J.A. Symons" by P. H. Muir (First Part)

1955

The Book Collector, Winter 1954

Journal
Includes "Bibliomanes I: A.J.A. Symons" by P. H. Muir (Second Part)

The Book Collector, Summer 1955

Journal
Includes "Bibliomanes I: A.J.A. Symons by P. H. Muir" (Third Part)

The Book Collector, Autumn 1955

Journal
Includes "Bibliomanes II: Sir Hugh Walpole" by Percy H. Muir (First Part)

The Quest for Corvo

A.J.A. Symons
Introduction by Julian Symons
Cassell. Boards with dust jacket

The Book Collector, Winter 1955

Journal
Includes "Bibliomanes II: Sir Hugh Walpole by Percy H. Muir" (Second Part)

1956

The Book Collector, Spring 1956

Journal
Includes "Bibliomanes II: Sir Hugh Walpole" by Percy H. Muir (Third Part)

Minding My Own Business

Percy Muir
Chatto & Windus. Blue cloth with dust jacket

Printer and Playground

Oliver Simon
Faber & Faber. Boards with dust jacket

1957

The Eye of the Beholder

Lance Sieveking
Hutton. Cloth with pictorial dust jacket

By Request: An Autobiography

André L. Simon
The Wine and Food Society. Blue buckram with dust jacket

1962

Oscar Wilde and His Literary Circle: A Catalog of Manuscripts and Letters in the William Andrews Clark Memorial Library

Compiled by John Charles Finzi
University of California Press. Cloth with dust jacket

1963

The Private Library, First Series, Vol. 4, No. 7, July 1963

Journal
Includes "How I Became a Book Collector" by Desmond Flower

1964

Museum Piece

James Laver
Houghton Mifflin. Boards with pictorial dust jacket

1966

Long Shadows

Shane Leslie
John Murray. Cloth with pictorial dust jacket

1967

A Bibliography of Frederick Rolfe Baron Corvo

Cecil Woolf
Rupert Hart-Davis. Red cloth with dust jacket

Drink and Be Merry

Vyvyan Holland
Michael Joseph. Boards with decorated dust jacket

1968

The Private Library, Second Series, Vol. 1, No. 1, Spring 1968

Journal
Includes "The Book-Collector's Quarterly" by Desmond Flower

An Evergreen Garland

Vyvyan Holland
Cassell. Boards with dust jacket

1969

In the Twilight

André L. Simon
Michael Joseph. Brown cloth with dust jacket

1971

My Lives

Francis Meynell
Random House. Cloth

1972

Stanley Morison

Nicolas Barker
Macmillan. Red cloth with dust jacket

1973

Song and Words: A History of the Curwen Press

Herbert Simon
David R. Godine. Blue cloth with decorative dust jacket

1975

Some Letters to A.J.A. Symons

Vincent O'Sullivan
Tragara Press. Wrappers
Limited to 130 copies

1978

The Private Library, Third Series, Vol. 1, No. 1, Spring 1978

Journal
Includes "The Book-Collector's Quarterly 1930-1933" by Desmond Flower

1980

Rules Rolls and Records of The Double Crown Club

Hugh Williamson
Stinehour Press. Quarter black cloth

1981

Antiquarian Book Monthly Review, Vol. 8, No. 10, Issue 90, October 1981

Magazine
Includes "A.J.A. Symons Part I: The First Edition Club" by George Sims

Antiquarian Book Monthly Review, Vol. 8, No. 11, Issue 91, November 1981

Magazine
Includes "A.J.A. Symons Part II: Brother Speculator" by George Sims

1985

The Book Collector, Autumn 1985

Journal
Includes "A.J.A. Symons: Brother Speculator" by Julian Symons

A.J.A. Symons: Brother Speculator

Julian Symons
Pamphlet
Talk delivered to the Double Crown Club on October 18, 1984
Reprinted from *The Book Collector,* Autumn 1985 issue, for presentation to members of the Double Crown Club

The Rare Book Game

George Sims
Holmes Publishing. Black cloth with dust jacket
Limited to 650 signed copies

1986

A.J.A. Symons: His Life and Speculations

Julian Symons
Oxford University Press. Paperback
Includes "Afterword, Thirty Years On" by Julian Symons

The Company We Kept

Barbara Kaye

Werner Shaw & Elkin Mathews. Paper boards with dust jacket

1987

André Simon: Gourmet and Wine Lover

Patrick Morrah

Constable. Boards with dust jacket

1988

George Moore on Parnassus: Letters (1900-1933)

Helmut E. Gerber

University of Delaware Press. Cloth with dust jacket

1989

Jigsaw

Sybille Bedford

Hamish Hamilton. Paper boards with dust jacket

Edward Wadsworth: A Painter's Life

Barbara Wadsworth

Michael Russell. Paper boards with dust jacket

Christopher Sclater Millard (Stuart Mason): Bibliographer and Antiquarian Book Dealer

H. Montgomery Hyde

Global Academic Publishers. Cloth with dust jacket

Limited to 500 copies

The Biographer's Art

Edited by Jeffrey Meyers

New Amsterdam Books. Boards with dust jacket

Includes "A.J.A. Symons's *The Quest for Corvo*" by A.O.J. Cockshut

1991

Fellows in Foolscap: Memoirs of a Publisher

Desmond Flower

Robert Hale. Boards with dust jacket

A.J.A Symons 1900-1941: An Anniversary Catalogue

Notes and Comments by Julian Symons
Stone Trough Books
Catalogue
Limited to 400 copies

David Tennant and the Gargoyle Years

Michael Luke
Weidenfeld & Nicolson. Boards with pictorial dust jacket

1994

Book and Magazine Collector, No. 119, February 1994

Magazine
Includes "A.J.A. Symons: Biographer and Book Collector Extraordinaire" by Richard Dalby

A Life in Catalogues and Other Essays

George Sims
Holmes Publishing. Black cloth with pictorial dust jacket
Limited to 650 copies

1996

Julian Symons: A Bibliography

John Walsdorf
Oak Knoll Press & St. Paul's Bibliographies. Boards

Modern Literature including Books and Manuscripts from the Library of Julian Symons: Catalogue 1216

Maggs Bros. Catalogue

2005

The Society's Other Founder

Offprint from International Wine & Food Society website

2008

From Sickert to Gertler: Modern British Art from Boxted House

Alice Strang
National Gallery of Scotland. Card

2009

Baron Corvo: From the Collection of Donald Weeks

Maggs Brothers.
Catalogue
Limited to 100 copies

Shane Leslie: Sublime Failure

Otto Rauchbauer
Lilliput Press. Paper boards with dust jacket

2012

IWFS History

Offprint from The Wine and Food Society of Boston website

2013

Wilde Discoveries: Traditions, Histories, Archives

Joseph Bristow (editor)
University of Toronto Press. Boards with dust jacket

Airborne: Scenes from the Life of Lance Sieveking

Paul Sieveking
Strange Attractor Press. Boards with pictorial dust jacket
Limited to 250 copies

Raven: The Turbulent World of Baron Corvo

Robert Scoble
Strange Attractor Press. Boards with pictorial dust jacket

2014

The Corvo Cult: The History of an Obsession

Robert Scoble
Strange Attractor Press. Boards with pictorial dust jacket

2016

Edward Bawden – Scrapbooks

Brian Webb and Peyton Skipwith.
Lund Humphries. Pictorial boards

2018

The Quest for Corvo: An Experiment in Biography

A.J.A. Symons
Introduction by Mark Valentin
Tartarus Press. Boards with pictorial dust jacket
Limited to 300 copies

VI

CHECKLIST OF THE EXHIBITION

Background of A.J.A. Symons

1. A.J.A. Symons aged about 16 with his siblings

London

Photograph

Photograph showing a young Symons and his siblings in a garden, likely the garden of Mount Lebanon, Cedars Road, Clapham, London. The house has since been demolished.

The picture shows (from left to right) Julian (later a crime writer and Symons's own biographer), Edith, Alphonse ("AJ"), Stanley, and Morris and seems likely to have been taken around 1916, when Symons would have been about 16.

2. A.J.A. Symons, aged 18

London

Photograph

Studio portrait by Elsee Studios of Clopham Junction. The back of the mount is marked "Age 18, while in the army," dating the photograph to 1918–1919.

3. Symons with ex-King Manoel of Portugal and others at the opening of the new Clubhouse of The First Edition Club at 17 Bedford Square on May 15, 1928

London

Photograph

Photograph of Symons (then aged 27) in morning dress together with (from left to right) Dr. George Williamson (Chairman of the Club) ex-King Manoel, and Lord Vaux of Harrowden at the opening of the exhibition of Selected Examples of Modern English Private Presses.

4. Julian Symons

A.J.A. Symons: His Life and Speculations

London

Oxford University Press 1985
The image of Symons was originally included in *Thirty Personalities and a Self-portrait: Lithographs by (Percy) Wyndham Lewis* (1932).

5. A.J.A. Symons considering a glass of wine
London
Photograph 1930s
Likely taken in the thirties during Symons's involvement with the Wine and Food Society.

6. Symons on holiday
Photograph 1930s
Photograph of Symons leaning on a country gate. Photograph noted on its back as "in camp staying with John Black in his caravan." John E. Black was an attendee of the second Corvine banquet.

7. Howard Costner

Portrait of Symons
London
Photograph 1940
One of a series of six photographs taken by Howard Costner in 1940, when Symons was already ill. The original is © National Portrait Gallery, London.

Calligraphy

8. A.J.A. Symons

Letter to Mrs. Leonard Cohen
London
Manuscript 1924
Calligraphic letter on First Edition Club letterhead dated October 7, 1924, explaining the difficulties Symons had had in obtaining the signatures of the lenders to the Club's First Loan Exhibition held at Mrs. Cohen's house at 27 Sussex Square, London, in December 1922.

9. A.J.A. Symons

List of the signatures of lenders to the First Loan Exhibition
London

Manuscript 1924

A calligraphic list of signatures referred to in the item above with a particularly elaborate heading. The list includes both Max Judge and Symons, the co-founders of the Club.

10. A.J.A. Symons
Letter to PJ

London

Manuscript 1924–28

Calligraphic letter on First Edition Club letterhead postponing a meeting and with a pen drawing by Symons of how to bring Harold to the meeting. "PJ" is likely Percy James Davis, a member of the Outspoken Debating Society, a discussion group that included Symons. Davis was a solicitor, and his firm, Bullcraig & Davis, was to represent Symons' estate. "Harold" is Captain Harold Fisher MC, a lifelong friend of Symons and also a member of the Society, who lived in Balham, South London. The meeting referred to was likely of the Society.

11. A.J.A. Symons
Letter to Lytton Strachey

Manuscript 1928

Calligraphic letter from Symons on First Edition Club stationery dated July 17, 1928, presenting his *Emin: The Governor of Equitoria* to Strachey.

12. A.J.A. Symons
Letter to Sciolist (Ivor Stewart-Liberty)

London

Manuscript 1927

Typed letter on First Edition Club letterhead to Sciolist dated September 12, 1927. Sciolist was the title taken by Ivor Stewart-Liberty as a member of the Sette of Odd Volumes. The letter is signed with Symons's initials, beneath which Symons has written SPECULATORROTALUCEPS, which was his own title, Speculator, spelled forward and backward. The reference to *Irish Wine* in the letter is to the printing of Maurice Healy's paper of the same title as Opusculum No. 84 of the Sette of Odd Volumes.

13. A.J.A. Symons
Letter to Mr. J. R. Biggs

London
Manuscript 1929
Calligraphic letter on First Edition Club letterhead to Mr. J. R. Biggs of the School of Art, Derby, dated October 3, 1929, critiquing a copy of a magazine Biggs had sent Symons. Biggs designed and executed several of the bindings included in the Club's exhibition of post-war English bookbindings in 1931. Symons, in his review of that exhibition included in *The Book-Collector's Quarterly*, Number XIII, noted that Biggs's "execution fell below the quality of his designs."

14. A.J.A. Symons
Letter to Mr. E. Joseph

London
Manuscript 1936
Calligraphic letter on Symons's personal 6 Little Russell Street letterhead dated February 18, 1936, to a Mr. Joseph, confirming a meeting and with the closing "yours in Corvo," the "in Corvo" apparently added as an afterthought. Paul's Bake House Court was a street near St. Paul's Cathedral in London.

15. A.J.A. Symons
Letter to Lady Swaythling

London
Manuscript 1938
Calligraphic letter to Lady Swaythling on Symons's personal 6 Little Russell Street letterhead dated May 26, 1938, thanking her for the gift of one of the 25 large paper copies of Oscar Wilde's *The Sphinx* published by Elkin Mathews and John Lane at the Bodley Head in 1894 with a cover design and plates by Charles Ricketts.
Lady Swaythling (1879–1965) was the second member of the Wine and Food Society and a member of its Council.

16. A.J.A. Symons
Letter to Edward Wadsworth

Finchingfield

Manuscript 1940

Letter on plain paper dated December 12, 1940, to the artist Edward Wadsworth (1889–1949) thanking Wadsworth for the gift of a book illustrating his work. Later in the letter, Symons explains the "calligraphic deterioration" of the letter by noting that he had mislaid his pen, and that it was due to "muscular weakness, not drink!"

The First Edition Club

17. Objects and Rules of The First Edition Club, 17 Pall Mall East

London
The First Edition Club 1922
The initial Objects and Rules of the Club showing the composition of the initial Committee, none of whom, except Symons himself, would still be on the Committee the following year. The annual subscription was set at 10/6, with an entrance fee of 10/6.

18. Prospectus for The First Edition Club, 17 Pall Mall East

London
The First Edition Club 1922
The initial prospectus of the Club, printed by the Morland Press, with an essay on the virtues of a first edition. It notes that the entrance fee is now one guinea, with an annual subscription of 10/6, indicating this prospectus was issued subsequent to the previous item. This copy bears the book label of George Sims, the great British post-WWII rare book seller, who handled many books from Symons's library as a result of his friendship with Julian Symons.

19. Objects and Rules of The First Edition Club, 69 Great Russell Street, 1923

London
The First Edition Club 1923
The Objects and Rules of the Club printed at the Curwen Press following its first move from Pall Mall East to Great Russell Street, showing the composition of the revised Committee. The annual subscription was now set at one guinea but with no entrance fee. The Club soon moved to 6 Little Russell Street.

20. Prospectus for The First Edition Club, Bedford Square

London

The First Edition Club 1928

The Prospectus printed for the Club by the Curwen Press on its move from Little Russell Street to 17 Bedford Square. The prospectus includes a short history of the Club (which makes no mention of Max Judge, the co-founder of the Club with Symons, although he is included in Benefactors as having housed the Club) and lists of former and current Committee members, Benefactors, exhibitions held by the Club, and Publications of the Club through May 1928.

21. A.J.A. Symons

Proposals for enlargement of The First Edition Club

London

First Edition Club 1927

The prospectus issued by the Club in connection with its proposed acquisition of a house at 100 Great Russell Street. Owing to its cost, this purchase was not completed and the Club instead took the lease of 17 Bedford Square. This copy from the collection of the Grolier Club.

22. The First Edition Club limited issue of 1,500 debentures of £10 each

London

The First Edition Club 1927

One of an issuance of £15,000 of debentures issued in November 1927 in connection with the Club's acquisition of the lease of 17 Bedford Square. The debenture is signed by Dr. George Williamson as Chairman of the Club, and twice by Symons as both a Director and Secretary. The debenture is annotated "A first and final distribution of 1s in the £1 has been made on this Debenture. 4th April 1933," reflecting the loss on liquidation of the Club.

23. Menu card for the 1929 Annual Reunion Dinner

London

The First Edition Club 1929

The Club held annual dinners for its members, and the 1929 dinner was held on December 5, 1929, with Michael Sadleir in the Chair. Toasts were proposed by Osbert Sitwell, Francis Meynell, and Desmond

MacCarthy, and responses were made by Michael Sadleir, Commander Oliver Lockyer-Lampson, DSO, MP, and Symons, respectively.

24. Letter to members, 9 March 1931

London
The First Edition Club 1931
Typed letter on First Edition Club letterhead proposing to Mr. Leon D Becker, editor of *Fuel Oil Journal*, who had only been elected a member in February 1931, that members contribute £10 each to liquidate the Club's debt. The letter states that the Club has been accepted "by book collectors all over the world as the European equivalent of the Grolie Club of New York."

25. Letter to members, March 31, 1932

London
The First Edition Club 1931
Form letter from 17 Bedford Square to Mr. Leon D. Becker advising that the Club was to be extricated from its financial difficulties and would move back to its former premises at 6 Little Russell Street where "we shall be living within our means." The letter is addressed and signed by Symons.

26. Percy J. Smith

New premises of The First Edition Club at 6 Little Russell Street London W.C.

Included in *The Book-Collector's Quarterly*, Number V
London
Cassell & Co. 1932
Published in connection with the Club's return from 17 Bedford Squar to its former premises in Little Russell Street, following the Club liquidation and resumption. Percy Smith (1882–1948) was an Englis calligrapher and engraver, and author of *Lettering: A Handbook of Moder Alphabets* (1936) and *Civic and Memorial Lettering* (1946). His *Letterin A Plea* was issued in 1932 as the 20th publication of the Club, and a exhibition of his typographical work was held by the Club in 1935.

27. A.J.A. Symons

Bibliographical Catalogue of the First Loan Exhibition – Prospectus

London

The First Edition Club 1922

Prospectus for the catalogue written by Symons of the Club's first exhibition, comprising books loaned by members. The exhibition was held over two days only and, optimistically, 500 copies were to be printed for members. The price was announced as one guinea.

28. William Hazlitt

Reply to Z – Prospectus

London

The First Edition Club 1923

Prospectus for *A Reply to Z*, a hitherto unpublished manuscript by William Hazlitt, issued as the second publication of the Club. Three hundred copies were to be printed by the Curwen Press. The price was announced as 21 shillings (one guinea).

29. G. S. Tomkinson

A Select Bibliography and History of the Principal Modern Presses Public and Private in Great Britain and Ireland – Prospectus

London

The First Edition Club 1924

Prospectus for *A Select Bibliography* written by Mr. G. S. Tomkinson issued as the fifth publication of the Club. One thousand copies were to be printed by the Curwen Press. The binding was announced as full buckram; however, the published book is bound in cloth-backed boards. The price was two guineas.

30. Ambrose Bierce

Ten Tales-Prospectus

London

The First Edition Club 1924

Prospectus for *Ten Tales* by Ambrose Bierce, with an introduction by Symons, issued as the eighth publication of the Club. These stories had not previously been printed in Great Britain. The edition was to be limited to 500 copies printed at the Curwen Press at a price of fifteen shillings.

31. Ambrose Bierce
Battle Sketches-Prospectus

London

The First Edition Club 1930

Prospectus for *Battle Sketches* by Ambrose Bierce, issued as the 17th publication of the Club. The book was designed by Basil Newdigate and printed at his Shakespeare Head Press as the third in a series of books to be printed by eminent English typographers. The edition was to be limited to 350 copies. The price was set at two pounds, ten shillings.

32. Ambrose Heal
The English Writing-Masters and their Copy-Books 1570–1800 – Prospectus

London

The First Edition Club 1931

Prospectus for *The English Writing-Masters and their Copy-Books 1570–1800* by Ambrose Heal, issued as the 19th publication by the Club. The book was printed in an edition of 300 copies by Cambridge University Press, of which 100 were numbered and bound for Club members. The price was five guineas.

33. A.J.A. Symons
An Announcement Regarding a New Series of Books

London

The First Edition Club 1928

Announcement of a series of books to be printed by distinguished British printers including John Johnson (Oxford University Press), Oliver Simon (Curwen Press), Basil Newdigate (Shakespeare Head Press), and Francis Meynell (Nonesuch Press). The last book announced, a biography of Talleyrand by Herbert Trench to be printed by Francis Meynell, was not issued.

34. A.J.A. Symons

A Bibliography of the Works of the Writers and Book Illustrators of the Eighteen-nineties with Short Biographies

London

The First Edition Club 1926

The prospectus for Symons's proposed bibliography of 41 writers active in the 1890s. Announced for publication by the Club in 1926, with a dummy binding prepared and a number of sections set up in type. The book was to have included approximately 700 pages, and to have been printed under the supervision of Oliver Simon and bound in half pigskin. The price was to be five guineas. Publication was again announced in 1931 (through *The Book-Collector's Quarterly*, Number II), now in three volumes at a price of six guineas, but Symons was ultimately unable to find a publisher for this work.

35. A.J.A. Symons

An Announcement of Some Good Books from The First Edition Club 1936–37

London

The First Edition Club 1936

Announcement of nine books to be issued by the Club, of which only the first two (*Letters from Aubrey Beardsley to Leonard Smithers* and *The Songs of Meleager)* were actually issued by the Club. The books not issued included *Rolfe at Holywell* and *A Bibliography of the Writings of George Moore* by Symons. The announcement notes that good binding was to be a feature of these books.

First Edition Club Catalogues

36. Catalogue of some manuscripts and early printed books – Illustrating "The Art of Good Living"– from the collection of André L. Simon

London

The First Edition Club 1931

Catalogue of the exhibition held at 17 Bedford Square in January 1931 of books from the collection of Symons's great friend, and co-founder with Symons of the Saintsbury Club and the Wine and Food Society.

Introduction by H. Warner Allen (1881–1968), a then-leading wine writer. Printed at the Pelican Press.

37. Exhibition of Modern Manuscript Books by the Society of Scribes & Illuminators & Others

London

The First Edition Club 1931

Opening speech to the exhibition held at 17 Bedford Square in May 1931 by Graily Hewitt. Graily Hewitt (1864–1952) was a calligrapher considered by some as second only to Edward Johnson in the early 20th-century revival of calligraphy in Great Britain. He was the author of *The Pen and Type-Design*, the 14th publication of the Club.

38. Post-War English Bookbindings

London

The First Edition Club 1934

Catalogue of the exhibition held at 6 Little Russell Street in January 1934. In addition to bindings by Kenneth Hobson of Henry T. Wood Ltd. and George Fisher at the Gregynog Press Bindery, etc., there are bindings executed by J. R. Biggs of the School of Art, Derby (see calligraphic letter from Symons #13 above), and two bindings (*Salammbo* and *The Complete Poetical Works of Shelley*) designed by Symons himself and executed by Henry T. Wood Ltd. See below, #97.

39. Catalogue of an Exhibition of Books Printed in the U.S.S.R. in the Period 1930–1936

London

The First Edition Club 1936

Catalogue of the exhibition held at 6 Little Russell Street in November–December 1936. The exhibition was opened by Ivan Maisky (1884–1975), the Russian Ambassador to the Court of St. James in the period 1932–1943.

40. A.J.A. Symons

Fifty Books of the Year 1932

London

The First Edition Club 1933

Catalogue of the fifth annual exhibition held at 6 Little Russell Street

The exhibitions were based on the series launched in the U.S. in 1923 by the American Institute of Graphic Arts, and were intended to encourage good book production. The cover of the catalogue encourages good binding. Introduction by Symons, who remarks that there was little sign that the quality of bindings was improving. One of the books on the list is *Dean Swift's Library* by Harold Williams, a member of the Selection Committee.

41. A.J.A. Symons
Fifty Books of the Year 1935
London
The First Edition Club 1936
Catalogue of the eighth annual exhibition held at 6 Little Russell Street. The exhibition was opened by the artist Albert Rutherston (1881–1953). Introduction by Symons, who notes a significant improvement over prior years, particularly in binding.

42. A.J.A. Symons
Fifty Books of the Year 1936
London
The First Edition Club 1937
Catalogue of the ninth annual exhibition held at 6 Little Russell Street. The exhibition was opened by the bibliophile Holbrook Jackson (1874–1948). Introduction by Symons, who notes continued improvement. Included in the list is *The Nonesuch Century* by Symons, Desmond Flower, and Francis Meynell.

43. A.J.A. Symons
Fifty Books of the Year 1937
London
The First Edition Club 1938
Catalogue of the tenth annual exhibition held at 6 Little Russell Street. The exhibition was opened by the novelist and book collector Sir Hugh Walpole (1884–1941). Introduction by Symons, who draws particular attention to *Cecil Beaton's Scrapbook* for its "unconventional settings and use of numerous titlings, well suited to its miscellaneous contents."

44. Invitation to Submit a Book for Consideration as one of the Fifty Books of the Year for 1938

Form letter. The letter requests two copies of each book selected: one for the Club's files and one copy for exhibition in America. The letter notes that "The Club is particularly anxious to encourage the better production of ordinary trade books."

45. A.J.A. Symons
Fifty Books of the Year 1938

London
The First Edition Club 1939
Catalogue of the 11th and final annual exhibition held at 6 Little Russell Street. The exhibition was opened by the writer Shane Leslie (1885–1971). Introduction by Symons, who notes that the inclusion of more printers and publishers than previous years demonstrates the widespread improvement in book-production.

The Sette of Odd Volumes

46. The Lay of the Odd Volumes

London
The Sette of Odd Volumes 1938
From the booklet issued by the Sette in November 1938, during the presidency of Symons. "The Lay" was written by Wilsey Martin, with music by Paul Bevan. and was sung at meetings of the Sette. It was first performed in 1895. The chorus includes the refrain, "We are Odd, very Odd."

47. Rules of the Sette of Odd Volumes

London
The Sette of Odd Volumes 1938
From the booklet issued by the Sette in November 1938, during the presidency of Symons. The rules combine practical rules for the organization of the Sette with humorous rules such as Rule XVI, which states that "There shall be no Rule XVI," and Rule XVIII, which states that "No Odd Volume shall talk unasked on any subject he understands."

48. Menu Card for the 418th Meeting of the Sette

The Sette of Odd Volumes 1926
Symons (Speculator) delivered his paper on "Frederick Baron Corvo" at this meeting. The menu has Corvine references, and the front of the menu incorporates a Beardsleyesque pen drawing of a young lady dusting a set of books entitled OV (Odd Volumes).

49. Menu Card for the 428th Meeting of the Sette

The Sette of Odd Volumes 1927
Symons (Speculator) delivered his paper on "Emin: Governor of Equitoria" at this meeting. The card states that following Symons's delivery, "Any one who likes may then . . . call attention to as many of Brother Speculator's glaring mis-statements as the brevity of time will allow." The front of the menu incorporates a pen drawing of Emin by R. T. Gould (Hydrographer).

50. Menu of July 5 1930

A dinner held at the Lee Manor, Lee, the house of Ivor Stewart-Liberty (Sciolist), during Stewart-Liberty's term as President. The menu refers to Vyvyan Holland (Idler), Speculator (Symons), Sciolist (Stewart-Liberty), and Scribbler (Ralph Straus).

51. Menu Card for the 489th Meeting of the Sette, Installation Night

Roland Oliver (Fiddler) was installed as President or Oddshippe in succession to Leslie R. Ray (Athlete) at this meeting. The cover depicts members of the Sette, including Symons (front upper center) as Romans in an amphitheater watching the handover of a key by two athletes. Cartouches of the members, including that of Symons (Speculator) showing a pipe blowing smoke rings, are displayed. The picture is by John Hassall (Limner, and President in 1908).

52. Invitation to Attend the 430th Meeting of the Sette

London
The Sette of Odd Volumes 1928
Invitation to Leslie Chaundy, a bookseller, from Speculator (Symons) in Symons's calligraphic hand. The card notes that the Sette is "United once a month to form a perfect Sette," and that its objects are "Conviviality and Mutual Admiration."

53. Br. Sciolist (Ivor Stewart-Liberty)
Letter to Members of the Sette of Odd Volumes

London
Sette of Odd Volumes 1928
Letter from Stewart-Liberty (Sciolist and Acting Secretary) noting that one of the two primary objects of the Sette, mutual admiration, was not being practiced, and requesting that His Oddshippe be informed of any significant events occurring in the life of a member.

54. Charge Sheet for Ralph Straus

London
The Sette of Odd Volumes 1932
Spoof charge sheet for Ralph Straus (Scribbler). Straus was accused, among other things, of "being found by night in the Savoy Hotel in unlawful possession of writing implements." This copy was sent in a black envelope addressed by Symons.

55. Booklet for the 524th Meeting of the Sette: Ladies' Night 1937

London
The Sette of Odd Volumes 1937
Each year, a meeting of the Sette was designated as Ladies' Night and members were allowed to introduce female guests. The front of the elaborate menu augments the OV symbol of the Sette to spell LOV. The program notes that after the meal the "Odd Volumes' favorite sport – guest-baiting" will occur. Symons is listed as attending without a guest, one of only two of the twenty members present to do so.

Corvine Society/Saintsbury Club/Wine and Food Society

56. A.J.A. Symons
Menu Card for the First Corvine Banquet

London
Menu for the first Corvine Banquet held at the Ambassador Club in London on June 27, 1929.
The back cover bears the pencil signatures of all seventeen attendees including a particularly decorative signature by Symons and a bold signature by J. Maundy-Gregory, as well as the signature of the undisclosed "Magistr Magnus Soc. Conv."

57. A.J.A. Symons
A True Recital of the Procedure of the First Banquet held by the Corvine Society

London

Corvine Society 1929

Includes the menu and a report of the proceedings, lists the 17 attendees, and reproduces the speeches delivered by Shane Leslie, Symons, and Harry Pirie-Gordon. Symons noted the Corvo manuscripts on display. Professor Dawkins, Grant Richards, and Sholto Douglas also spoke, and Symons ends the report with the statement that after "larger and larger libations were poured more and more freely . . . the meeting did not so much end as deliquesce."

58. Frederick Baron Corvo
The Bull Against the Enemy of the Anglican Race

London

Corvine Society 1929

The first printing, in an edition of 50 copies, of this work written by Frederick Baron Corvo in 1908. *The Bull* is purportedly written by the fictitious Hadrian VII, the title of Corvo's best-known work, at the urging of Nicholas Crabbe, another fictional person created by Corvo who appeared in Corvo's *Nicholas Crabbe: or, The One and the Many* and *Desire and Pursuit of the Whole*. According to Symons in his "Check-List of Corvo" included in *Points: Second Series, 1866–1934*, it was excluded from Corvo's *Hadrian VII* owing to its libelous content. The work was printed for Symons by the Curwen Press and was distributed to attendees at the first Corvine Banquet. The manuscript was subsequently offered for sale by George Sims, who noted some discrepancies from the printed version.

59. A.J.A. Symons
A True Recital of the Procedure of the Second Banquet held by the Corvine Society

London

Corvine Society 1929

Held at the Ambassador Club on December 12, 1929. Includes the menu and a report of the proceedings, lists the 30 attendees, and reproduces the speeches delivered by Shane Leslie and Symons. Symons notes that membership is open to any student of Corvo, and that "The test of suitability is a formal examination paper, copies of which can be obtained on application to the Secretary, such applications to be made after an elaborate lunch or dinner provided by the prospective candidate." The report ends, "then the already dissipated company dispersed."

60. André L. Simon
The Saintsbury Club: A Scrapbook

Sonoma CA
The Rare Wine Co. 1993
This copy, a reprint of the original published in 1943, in an edition of 14c copies with an introduction by Merlin Holland, son of Vyvyan Holland and grandson of Oscar Wilde, and the essay "When Club Meets Club" by Symons, originally included in *Wine and Food*, No. 19 (1938). The book reports the menus and the wines drunk at each meeting.
This copy one of 50 issued to members of the Saintsbury Club.

61. Stephen Potter
Professor of Taste

London
Wilfred Meynell 1936
The Saintsbury Oration delivered by Stephen Potter (1900–69) the biographer and humorist at the Tenth Meeting of the Saintsbury Club on 23 April 1936. The booklet was printed for Wilfred Meynell at the Fanfare Press for presentation to members, and includes the seating plan for the dinner. This copy is inscribed at length by Potter to Clarissa Bell.

62. Prospectus for Wine & Food Society

London
The Wine and Food Society 1933
Prospectus for the Wine and Food Society issued as from 6 Little Russell Street, still the base for The First Edition Club. Includes "The Wine and Food Society Objects and Rules." Printed by the Curwen Press.

63. Menu Card for the Forty-Ninth Meeting (the Fourth Birthday Dinner)

London
The Wine and Food Society 1937
Held at the Langham Hotel over four evenings on October 28 and 29 and November 2 and 4. The dinner was repeated three times to accommodate the number of attendees from the rapidly growing Society. The notes include the statement that "Quiche Lorraine will probably be unfamiliar to most members." Printed by the Curwen Press. Manuscript correction likely in Symons's hand.

64. Menu Card for an Escoffier Dinner

London
The Wine and Food Society 1939
Dinner held at the Savoy Hotel over three evenings on April 19, 20, and 23, 1939, with André Simon, President, in the Chair. Likely printed by the Curwen Press.

65. Wine and Food: A Gastronomic Quarterly, Spring Number, 1934, No. 1

London
The Wine and Food Society 1934
The journal launched by the Wine and Food Society in 1934 under the editorship of André Simon, with Symons responsible for production and advertising. The first issue includes a review by Symons *of Madeira: Wine, Cakes and Sauce* by André Simon and Elizabeth Craig. The journal was published through 1970.

Works by Symons

66. A.J.A. Symons

A Bibliographical Catalogue of the First Loan Exhibition of Books and Manuscripts Held by The First Edition Club

London
The First Edition Club 1922
The first publication of the Club, limited to 500 copies printed by the Curwen Press. Symons inscribed this copy "For Mrs. Leonard Cohen this copy containing the signatures of the contributors to the exhibition

– 1922." Mrs. Cohen had made her house at 27 Sussex Square, London available for the exhibition. In his *Points: Second Series 1866–1934*, the bookseller Percy Muir notes this volume as "quite a useful scrapbook of information."

67. A.J.A. Symons
A Bibliography of the First Editions of Books by William Butler Yeats

London
The First Edition Club 1924
The third publication of The First Edition Club, limited to 500 copies printed by the Curwen Press. The catalogue of the Club's second exhibition was written by Symons, who inscribed this copy "For Charles Whibley with the cordial compliments of the compiler." Charles Whibley had provided the introduction to The First Edition Club's edition of Hazlitt's *A Reply to Z*, the second publication of the Club. Percy Muir's view of this volume in his *Points: Second Series 1866–1934* was that it "needs considerable supplementing to make it adequate."

68. A.J.A. Symons
A Bibliography of the First Editions Proofs and Manuscripts of Books by Lord Byron

Exhibited at the Fourth Exhibition held by The First Edition Club
January 1925
London
The First Edition Club 1925
The fifth publication of The First Edition Club, limited to 500 copies printed by the Curwen Press.
Symons inscribed this copy to his lifelong friend Captain Harold Fisher "HF from AJ."

69. A.J.A. Symons
An Anthology of "Nineties" Verse

London
Elkins Mathews & Marrot Ltd. 1928.
This copy inscribed by Symons "To Lady Swaythling in grateful tribute to her energy, wisdom, sympathy and generosity: in warm remembrance

of *The Sphinx* and the great period where it was printed, in which these yellow blooms grew from A.J.A. Symons June 1938." Lady Swaythling had given Symons a copy of Oscar Wilde's *The Sphinx*.

70. A.J.A. Symons
Baron Corvo

London
The Sette of Odd Volumes 1927
Privately printed opuscula of the Sette of Odd Volumes, Number 81. Limited to 199 copies printed by the Curwen Press of which 17 copies were printed on hand-made paper, were bound in blue morocco, and included a page of Corvo's handwriting as frontispiece. This copy, one of the 17, is inscribed to Holbrook Jackson by Symons. This is the paper on Corvo delivered by Symons at the 418th meeting of the Sette in November 1926, and was the forerunner to Symons's *The Quest for Corvo* published in 1934.

71. A.J.A. Symons
Baron Corvo

London
The Sette of Odd Volumes 1927
Privately printed opuscula of the Sette of Odd Volumes, Number 81. Limited to 199 copies printed by the Curwen Press. This is one of the 182 ordinary copies.
Copy number 71, inscribed by Symons to C.J.F. Jarchow.

72. A.J.A. Symons
Frederick Baron Corvo

Life and Letters, Vol. 1, No. 2, July 1928
London
Journal edited by Desmond MacCarthy. Hardback edition limited to 200 copies. Includes an amended version of Symons's paper on Corvo delivered to the Sette of Odd Volumes.

73. A.J.A. Symons
Emin: The Governor of Equitoria

London

The Fleuron 1928
Limited to 300 copies printed by the Curwen Press.
This copy inscribed by Symons "For his Oddshippe E. Heron Allen
before whom this prose fable was intrepidly read by the Speculator
OV." Speculator was the title assumed by Symons as a member of the
Sette of Odd Volumes, hence "OV."

74. A.J.A. Symons
Edgar Allen Poe

Life and Letters, Vol. 2, No. 10, March 1929
London
Journal edited by Desmond MacCarthy. Includes "Edgar Allen Poe" by
Symons. This paper was first read to the Sette of Odd Volumes at its
439th Meeting in February 1929.

75. A.J.A. Symons
An Episode in the Life of the Queen of Sheba

London
A.J.A. Symons and Albert Ehrman 1929
Privately printed for Albert Ehrman and Symons (likely by the Curwen
Press), limited to 150 copies. Inscribed by Symons "To Peter Burra with
the good wishes of AJAS."
This, Symons's only work of fiction, was prepared for Ladies' Night
at the Sette of Odd Volumes in 1929. Albert Ehrman owned the
Broxbourne Library of early printed books.

76. A.J.A. Symons
Tradition in Biography

Tradition and Experiment in Present-day Literature
London
Oxford University Press 1929
Comprises lectures delivered to the City Literary Institute in London
in 1929 by Symons and, among others, Edmund Blunden, T. S. Eliot,
Edith Sitwell, and Rebecca West.
This copy, a second impression, inscribed by Symons to "Geoffrey
Hobson from one of the experimenters A.J.A. Symons."

77. A.J.A. Symons
An Episode in the Life of the Queen of Sheba

Farrago, Number 3, October 1930
Oxford
Simon Nowell-Smith 1930
Edited by Peter Burra.
Includes "*An Episode in the Life of the Queen of Sheba*" by Symons.

78. A.J.A. Symons
H. M. Stanley

London
Duckworth 1933
This copy inscribed by Symons to "A. Ehrman, with cordial regards from his friend the author A.J. May 19, 1933."

79. A.J.A. Symons
The Quest for Corvo: An Experiment in Biography

London
Cassell & Co. 1934
Printed by the Curwen Press. Symons is best known for this book, which has been described as one of the seminal biographies of the twentieth century. It was groundbreaking in that it combined a description of Symons's search for Corvo with the biography of Corvo.
Elaborately inscribed by Symons to C. Bertrand Thompson, a pioneer in international management consulting.

80. Percy H. Muir
Points, Second Series, 1866–1934

London
Constable 1934
Limited to 750 copies on green paper and published by Constable.
Symons contributed "A Biographical Check-list of Baron Corvo" in which he describes the *True Recitals* of the Corvine Banquets as "having shed much new light, in truly Corvine fashion, on the extraordinary life of that extraordinary man." Percy Muir comments on Symons's *Catalogue of the First Loan Exhibition* and *A Bibliography of the First*

Editions of Books by William Butler Yeats. Symons himself reviewed this book in *The Book-Collector's Quarterly*, No. XVI.

81. A.J.A. Symons
Is It Wise?

Tallahassee
Fonthill Press 1979
The poem is a comment on the T. J. Wise forgery scandal. Limited to "about 125 copies" and printed as a keepsake for The Typophiles Christmas Luncheon.
Reprint of the original issued in an edition of 25 copies in the series of eight leaflets entitled *Weppons of Peace* by Philip Gosse in 1934. The leaflets were written by visitors to Weppons, Gosse's house in Sussex Symons also published an essay on "The Nineteenth Century Forgers" in *The Book-Collector's Quarterly*, Number XVI, in 1934.

82. Nancy Quennel (editor)
Epicure's Anthology of Banqueting Delights – Prospectus

London
Golden Cockerel Press 1936
Symons was to provide the introductory essay on "The Epicure and the Epicurian."

83. A.J.A. Symons
Inaugural Address of His Oddshippe Br. A.J.A. Symons (Speculator)

London
The Sette of Odd Volumes 1938
Booklet 54 of the Sette. Reproduces the speech given by Symons on his installation as President (Oddshippe) at its 525th Meeting on October 18 1938. In the speech, Symons explains his selection of the title Speculator Symons served as President for 1938–39.

84. A.J.A. Symons
Theodore Hook

English Wits: Their Lives and Jests
London

Hutchinson 1953

Edited by Leonard Russell, and first published by Hutchinson in 1941. Symons contributed a chapter on Theodore Hook (1778–1841), best known for the Berners Street Hoax of 1810, in which Hook won a bet that he could make any house in London the most talked-about house in London within a week. This copy a third impression published in 1953.

35. A.J.A. Symons
Wilde at Oxford

Horizon, Vol. 3, No. 16, April 1941
London 1941
Journal edited by Cyril Connolly. Includes "Wilde at Oxford" by Symons. According to item 70 in G. F. Sims's *Books and Manuscripts Including Some from the Collection of the Late A.J.A. Symons*, Catalogue 29, Connolly wrote to Symons that Augustus John, the painter who knew Wilde, had commented on how Symons had captured Wilde exactly.

36. A.J.A. Symons
The Diner-Out

Horizon, Vol. 4, No. 22, October 1941
London 1941
Journal edited by Cyril Connolly. Includes "The Diner-Out," the conclusion of the article "Wilde at Oxford," published in April 1941 and part of the proposed but never completed biography of Wilde by Symons. "The Diner-Out" had originally been published in *Fords and Bridges* in 1936.

37. A.J.A. Symons
Essays and Biographies

London
Cassell & Co. 1969
Selected and with an introduction by Julian Symons.
Includes the completed chapters of the proposed biography of Wilde as well as other pieces, both published and unpublished.

88. Julian Symons
Two Brothers: Fragments of a Correspondence

Edinburgh
Tragara Press 1955
Edition limited to 130 copies. Correspondence between Julian Symons
and Symons, 1939–41.

89. A.J.A. Symons
One Lump or Two: Tea, Twinings and Edward Bawden with Limericks by A.J.A. Symons

Norfolk
Mainstone Press 2010
Introduced by Peyton Skipwith and published by Mainstone Press
Comprises a series of advertisements for Twinings Tea with Symons's
limericks illustrated by Edward Bawden
Edward Bawden RA (1903–89) was a graphic artist and painter.

90. Ambrose Heal
London Tradesmen's Cards of the XVIIIth Century

London
Batsford for The First Edition Club 1925
Printed by the Curwen Press. One hundred copies were specially bound
for members of the Club as the seventh publication issued by the Club
Ambrose Heal, who was Chairman of Heal's furniture manufacturing
and retail business, also wrote *English Writing-Masters and their Copy
Books, 1570–1800*, the 19th publication of the Club. This copy (#40) in
scribed to F. Sissons by Symons.

91. Twenty Letters to Conrad

London
The First Edition Club 1926
Letters to Joseph Conrad from eleven literary contemporaries with an
introduction by G. Jean-Aubrey. Printed by the Curwen Press in a
edition of 220 copies as the ninth publication of the Club. Include
letters from Arnold Bennett, Stephen Crane, John Galsworthy
Constance Garnett, Edward Garnett, George Gissing, James Gibbon
Huneker, Henry James, Rudyard Kipling, E.V. Lucas, and H.G. Wells

92. Alban Dobson
Bibliography of the First Editions of Published and Privately Printed Books and Pamphlets by Austin Dobson

London

The First Edition Club 1925

Printed in an edition of 500 copies by the Curwen Press as the eighth publication issued by the Club.

This volume was described by *Percy Muir in his Points: Second Series, 1886–1934* as "Admirable although not quite exhaustive." This copy was inscribed by Symons to Harold Fisher in an elaborate pen drawing for Xmas 1925.

93. Alban Dobson
Bibliography of the First Editions of Published and Privately Printed Books and Pamphlets by Austin Dobson

London

The First Edition Club 1925

Another copy was inscribed by Symons to Harold Fisher in 1941 to replace the above copy, which Fisher mistakenly believed that he had mislaid. The drawing is remarkably similar to that in the above copy.

94. Graily Hewitt
The Pen and Type-Design

London

The First Edition Club 1928

Printed by the Oxford University Press in an edition of 250 copies as the 14th publication issued by the Club. This copy inscribed "this is the Club copy" and signed by Symons.

95. Aubrey Beardsley
Letters from Aubrey Beardsley to Leonard Smithers

London

The First Edition Club 1937

With an introduction by R. A. Walker. Printed by the Chiswick Press in an unspecified limitation as the 24th (and last) publication of the Club. According to Julian Symons in *A.J.A. Symons: His Life and Speculations*, Walker disliked the form of the book.

96. Ernest Dowson
The Poetical Works

London
Cassell & Bodley Head 1934
Edited and with an introduction by Desmond Flower. This copy is one
of a few specially bound and stamped as "Bound for The First Edition
Club by Henry T. Wood Ltd. London." Symons had discovered a
notebook containing Dowson's poems and later sold it to Flower.

97. Percy Bysshe Shelley
The Complete Poetical Works

London
Oxford University Press 1904
This is one of a few (25 or 50, per Flower) copies specially bound for
members of The First Edition Club by Henry T. Wood, Ltd. and was
presented to Desmond Flower by R. B. Fishenden, then President of
the Double Crown Club, following a meeting of that club at which
Flower spoke on Symons's book-production. With transmittal letter
and the signature of Flower. The binding was designed by Symons
and an example was included in the Club's 1934 exhibition of Post-War
English Bookbindings.

98. Philip Gosse
The History of Piracy

London
Longmans, Longmans Green 1932
Inscribed by Gosse to Symons, noting that this copy was especially
bound by North. In 1932, The First Edition Club held an exhibition of
books and manuscripts relative to buccaneers and piracy from Philip
Gosse's collection, and Gosse's opening speech at that exhibition is
reproduced in *The Book-Collector's Quarterly*, No. IX.

99. A. G. Street
Farmer's Glory

London
Faber 1934

Illustrated by Gwendoline Raverat. This is one of a few copies specially bound for members of The First Edition Club. Bears Symons's bookplate designed by V. Le Campion.

100. A.J.A. Symons and Desmond Flower (co-editors)
The Book-Collector's Quarterly
London
Cassell & Co. 1931–35
The 17 numbers (all published) of *The Book-Collector's Quarterly*, which was co-edited by Symons and Desmond Flower. The first 16 numbers were financed and published by Cassell, which then withdrew, and the 17th number was paid for by the Club. An 18th number was announced but never issued. The first eight numbers were issued both in a limited edition of 100 copies (75 copies for Numbers VI–VIII) and an ordinary edition. Thereafter, only ordinary copies were issued.

Manuscripts and Books
from the Library of A.J.A. Symons

101. A.J.A. Symons
Notes on Wilde
Manuscript
Autograph notes by Symons, possibly notes of a conversation with Charles Ricketts. The facing leaf comprises a manuscript design of the title page for *Oscar Wilde: Recollections* (Nonesuch Press, 1932) initialed J.P.R. – the name assumed by Ricketts for that publication. This sheet was included (#269) in G. F. Sims's Catalogue 29, *Books and Manuscripts Including Some from the Collection of the Late A.J.A. Symons*.

102. A.J.A. Symons
Draft Sentences on Oscar Wilde
Manuscript
Three drafts of one sentence and one draft of a second sentence in Symons's hand on a single sheet. This illustrates the effort Symons put into his writing.

103. A.J.A. Symons
H. M. Stanley

Manuscript
Fair copy by Symons in calligraphic hand of the opening chapter o
H. M. Stanley in a foolscap notebook of ruled blue hand-made pape
Bears Symons's Mount Lebanon Library bookplate.

104. Gustave Flaubert
Bibliomania

Northwestern University Library 1929
Limited to 500 copies. This copy inscribed by Theodore Wesley Koc
(translator) to The First Edition Club with the Club bookplate pasted in

105. Francis Colchester-Wemyss
The Pleasures of the Table

London
Nisbit 1931
Sir Francis Colchester-Wemyss (1872–1954) was a member of the Counc
of the Wine and Food Society, and President of the Croquet Association
a game Symons enjoyed. This copy bears Colchester-Wemyss's bookplat
which has been annotated by the author to read "A.J.A. Symons from
Francis Colchester-Wemyss June 1934." Also bears Symons's paper Bric
House bookplate. Colchester-Wemyss contributed a memoir of a vis
by Symons to his house in 1937 to *Wine and Food*, Number *32*.

106. Ralph Hodgson
The Mystery and Other Poems

London
Flying Fame 1913
Ralph Hodgson (1871–1962) was an English poet who, together wit
Claud Lovat Fraser and Holbrook Jackson, founded the At the Sign
the Flying Flame private press in 1912. This copy, like a number of bool
in his collection, has been wrapped by Symons in Curzon Press pap
with a manuscript label on spine. This copy, a large paper copy wit
decorations hand-colored by Claud Lovat Fraser, is marked "Marc
1934" in Symons's hand at the back and bears his small paper Bric
House bookplate.

07. Books of the "Nineties": Catalogue 42
London
Elkin Mathews Ltd. 1932
This was the catalogue for the first and unsuccessful sale of Symons's library. According to Julian Symons, less than one third in value of the items were sold. Elkin Mathews had taken out an advertisement in *The Book-Collector's Quarterly*, Number V (January 1932), which stated that "the firm have in the press a catalogue of a very remarkable collection of first editions of authors of the 1890's."

08. Library of a Collector and Man of Letters: Catalogue 72
Takeley
P. H. Muir for Elkin Mathews Ltd. 1939
This was the catalogue of the second sale of Symons's library. Muir considered the sale a success.

09. Books and Manuscripts Including Some from the Library of the Late A.J.A. Symons
Catalogue 29
G. F. Sims (Rare Books) 1955
The catalogue notes, despite the title, that the majority of the books offered had come from Symons's collection.

10. A.J.A. Symons 1900–1941: An Anniversary Catalogue
York
Stone Trough Books 1991
Notes and comments by Julian Symons. Includes an illustration of a portrait of Symons by Natalie Sieveking and illustrations of Symons's bookplates.

11. Modern Literature Including Books and Manuscripts from the Library of Julian Symons: Catalogue 1216
London
Maggs Bros. Ltd. 1996
Includes a substantial portion of the Symons material that had been retained by Julian Symons.

112. Julian Symons
A.J.A. Symons: His Life and Speculations
London
Eyre & Spottiswoode 1950
The only full-length biography of Symons to date. It was reissued b
Oxford University Press as a paperback in 1986 with an "Afterword
Thirty Years On" by Julian Symons.

Books Inscribed by Symons

113. Richard le Gallienne
The Romantic Nineties
London
G.P. Putnam's Sons 1926
Inscribed by Symons "To Holbrook Jackson. For the inventor of th
Nineties who, by not patenting his discovery, enabled me to be its bib
liographer. A.J.A. Symons May 20, 1926. In memory also of Willian
Morris." Catalogue 29 from G. F. Sims includes (#199) a copy of Jack
son's *The Eighteen-Nineties* (1913) inscribed "A.J.A. Symons Bibliogra
pher of the Nineties from its Historian Holbrook Jackson."

114. A.J.A. Symons, Desmond Flower, and Francis Meynell
The Nonesuch Century
London
Nonesuch Press 1936
Limited to 750 copies. This copy inscribed by Symons "For Andre Si
mon in tribute to his love of books. Very cordially from his friend th
Appraiser A.J. Feb 19 1936."
Bookplate of Anthony Hobson.

115. A.J.A. Symons, Desmond Flower, and Francis Meynell
The Nonesuch Century
London
Nonesuch Press 1936
Another copy. This copy inscribed by Symons to Vyvyan Holland "Fc
Vyvyan, directing his particular attention to plates 1, 32 & 50. Affection
ately from his friend A.J." Also signed by Francis Meynell.
Bookplate of Stuart B. Schimmel by Reynolds Stone.

16. Fr. Rolfe Baron Corvo
Chronicles of the House of Borgia

London
Grant Richards 1901
Bears the bookplate designed for Symons by Valentin Le Campion
(1903–52), the Russian-born engraver whose engravings were exhibited
at The First Edition Club.

17. Edmund Gosse
Gossip in a Library

London
William Heinemann 1913
Bears Symons's Finchingfield white-on-black bookplate.

18. Felix Folio
Helicon Hill

London
Selwyn & Blount 1921
Bears Symons's small paper Brick House bookplate.
This copy initialed by Claud Lovat Fraser, who drew the decorations
for this book. Also includes Desmond Coke's bookplate, which Fraser
designed.

LIMITED TO 500 COPIES SET IN CASLON TYPES.
DESIGN & TYPOGRAPHY BY JERRY KELLY.